T0265803

Favorite Flies for

THE UPPER MIDWEST

50 Essential Patterns from Local Experts

JERRY DARKES

STACKPOLE
BOOKS

Essex, Connecticut
Blue Ridge Summit, Pennsylvania

STACKPOLE BOOKS

An imprint of The Globe Pequot Publishing Group, Inc.
64 South Main Street
Essex, CT 06426
www.globepequot.com

Distributed by NATIONAL BOOK NETWORK

British Library Cataloguing in Publication Information available

Library of Congress Cataloging-in-Publication Data
Names: Darkes, Jerry, author.
Title: Favorite flies for the Upper Midwest : 50 essential patterns from
    local experts / Jerry Darkes.
Other titles: 50 essential patterns from local experts
Description: Essex, Connecticut : Stackpole Books, [2024] | Includes index.
Identifiers: LCCN 2024027617 (print) | LCCN 2024027618 (ebook) | ISBN
    9780811774208 (cloth) | ISBN 9780811774215 (epub)
Subjects: LCSH: Flies, Artificial—Lake States. | Fly tying—Lake States. |
    Fly fishing—Lake States.
Classification: LCC SH451 .D3688 2024 (print) | LCC SH451 (ebook) | DDC
    688.7/9124—dc23/eng/20240621
LC record available at https://lccn.loc.gov/2024027617
LC ebook record available at https://lccn.loc.gov/2024027618

∞™ The paper used in this publication meets the minimum requirements of
American National Standard for Information Sciences—Permanence of Paper for
Printed Library Materials, ANSI/NISO Z39.48-1992.

This book is dedicated to the memory of the early fly pattern creators of the Upper Midwest. In particular to Rusty Gates for his lifelong contributions in fly tying and fly fishing and never-ending efforts for conservation and preservation of the Au Sable River and northern Michigan.

CONTENTS

FOREWORD

If you want to *know* the fishing in a new lake or river, you can read about it, watch videos, ogle pictures . . . but nothing will *describe* the fishing as well as the locally famous fly. A good fly reflects the unique character of the fish in a specific waterway, and often at a specific time of year. How is the fishing on a northern Michigan trout stream in late May? You can read all about that! There are videos, sure. And internet pictures aplenty. But you can just look at Rusty's Spinner, with its deer hair body and outstretched hackle-tip wings, and imagine that perfect mixed May spinner fall, three or four different mayflies bouncing at dusk, a big fish rising in front of the logjam across the river . . . and you trying to steady your heart rate. That fly describes it perfectly.

The evolution of many of the flies you're about to read about have occurred across *generations* of fly tiers. Some flies have jumped from one region to another. Undoubtedly Fran Betters's Usual—an Adirondack classic—served as some inspiration for the Dust Bunny. But they are no longer the same fly. The unique requirements of vastly different river systems with eerily similar names (the Ausable in New York . . . and the Au Sable in Michigan) meant that the high-floating Usual needed to float lower, more like an emerger, and—with its now laid-back wing—could even be fished as a wet fly.

The world is full of one-hit wonders and internet rabbit holes that lead anglers to either (a) very cheap flies or (b) the "best flies ever." But there's more to it than that. The vast majority of the really good flies, like the Usual and the Dust Bunny, are the result of a tier listening to the fishery. A fly tier doesn't impart style onto the fly . . . the river (or lake) does. And that is why this important book exists. Forget the "The Only 13 Flies You'll Ever Need" articles. That may keep it simple, but it's shortchanging not only your fishing, but also all that fly fishing has to offer. Fly fishing is a lifestyle composed of hobbies: photography, rod-building, collectibles, distance casting, literature. But the fly is the soul of it.

So, enjoy meeting some very good flies from my home region—I met some new ones myself.

Josh Greenburg
Grayling, Michigan
December 30, 2023

ACKNOWLEDGMENTS

With any project like this there are always many people to thank and the fear that you will forget someone. If this happens, please accept my sincere apologics. First of all, thank you to everyone who was willing to share fly patterns, recipes, and information. This book is about you and your contributions to fly fishing and fly tying in the Upper Midwest.

In particular, I would like to highlight Josh Greenberg, who was always willing to review and share information on trout dry-fly patterns and point out possible discrepancies in the origin of a particular fly. Josh was also kind enough to write the foreword for this book, and I truly appreciate his knowledge and expertise of the region along with the support of everyone at Gates Lodge.

Kendrick Chittock is a professional photographer who was kind enough to share his expertise to help me with the fly plate photos. His assistance made my work much easier and quicker.

To my longtime friend Kevin Feenstra, thank you for sharing several of your key fly designs and great photographs. Also, to Ann Miller for help with insect identification and photos. Both have excellent books that should be in the libraries of all Upper Midwest fly fishers. Also, to Craig Amacker and Mat Wagner for their contributions on the Driftless region.

To all the great anglers, guides, and tiers whose patterns were contributed, suggested, or borrowed: Craig Amacker, Bear Andrews, Jeff Blood, Charlie Chlysta, Blane Chocklett, Eric Corya, Larry Dahlberg, Pat Ehlers, Tanner Ehlers, Kelly Galloup, Matt Grajewski, Chuck Kraft, Ted Kraimer, Rick Kustich, Bob Linsenman, Jeff Liskay, Tommy Lynch, Russ Maddin, Ed McCoy, Tim Neal, Charlie Piette, Dennis Potter, Dave Pynczkowski, Matt Redmond, Jerry Regan, Ray Schmidt, Greg Senyo, Bill Sherer, Nate Sipple, and Matt Zudweg. I hope I have represented you, your work, and your influence accurately.

To Craig Amacker, Phil Cook, Dave Hurley, Jeff Liskay, Tommy Lynch, and Joe Wolthuis for additional contributing photos—thank you.

Finally, to *all* Upper Midwest fly anglers and fly tiers. This book could not have been written without your continuing interest and support.

The waters of the Upper Midwest allow anglers to pursue a wide assortment of gamefish with flies. Both coldwater and warmwater species are present. They can be targeted anywhere from the waters of the Great Lakes, to large rivers, to tiny creeks, and all points in between.

INTRODUCTION

Where or what exactly is the Upper Midwest? An online search gives several different views. Essentially, it is part of the United States that includes Illinois, Indiana, Iowa, Michigan, Minnesota, Ohio, and Wisconsin. Some maps also include Missouri, North Dakota, and South Dakota. To me it is primarily the states that touch the western portion of the Great Lakes: Lake Michigan, Lake Huron, Lake Superior, and most of Lake Erie. From a fishing aspect, we could say that southern Ontario is part of this, as the big lakes and several connecting waterways are shared by the US and Canada.

Traversing the area, it changes dramatically. The boreal forest in the north gives way to the deciduous forest as you move south. The deciduous forest turns to the prairie grasslands moving from east to west. In between there is farmland, as much of the area is supported by agriculture. There are large urban areas as well as extensive tracts of near wilderness. It is also an area of climatic extremes. Temperatures can vary from well below zero to over 100 degrees Fahrenheit depending on time of year and location.

The type of fly-fishing waters and fish species available also varies greatly. We can fish tiny creeks for wild trout, small ponds for bass and bluegill, large rivers for trout and smallmouth, on up to the open waters of giant lakes for apex predators like muskie and lake trout. As we will see, the flies and techniques to present them also vary greatly across this region.

The Upper Midwest played a significant role in the development of fly fishing as it is practiced today. We know that by the mid-1800s, wealthy "sports" began to adventure across the region and fly-fishing equipment was part of their gear. The rapids of the St. Marys River was a popular destination, with some trips continuing by steamer to the Nipigon River at the northwest corner of Lake Superior.

The famous lake-dwelling coaster brook trout, called "rock trout" back then, were abundant in northern Lake Huron and throughout Lake Superior. The largest brook trout ever recorded came from the Nipigon River in 1915. At 14½ pounds, it will likely never be topped. Nearly eliminated, by the late twentieth century coaster brook trout had made a notable recovery due to strict catch-and-keep regulations.

When the railroad reached into the northern tier of Michigan's lower peninsula in the later 1800s, the famed grayling rivers were opened to exploitation. Many notable anglers of the day such as Theodore Gordon made the trip from the Catskills to Grayling, Michigan, to sample this renowned fishery. Sadly, we know the final result of this and the Michigan grayling was extirpated by around 1910.

McCloud River rainbow trout were stocked into the Great Lakes in 1873 at Oscoda, Michigan. Subsequent stockings took place through the late 1800s and self-sustaining populations were established. Most rainbow populations in the Upper Midwest are migratory, moving from the big lakes to tributaries to spawn, hence we refer to them as steelhead, just like their oceangoing relatives. Today, there is natural reproduction of these fish as well as aggressive stocking programs. Fly fishing for steelhead

The coaster brook trout is a true Upper Midwest native that was found in Lake Superior and northern Lake Huron. The Province of Ontario has been successful in increasing populations in Lake Superior. In the US, the progress has been much slower.

Steelhead are a premier gamefish for Upper Midwest fly fishers. They are found in all five of the Great Lakes and connecting waters. There is substantial natural reproduction of steelhead across the lakes along with aggressive stocking programs.

contributes a significant amount to the sportfishing industry of the region.

Brown trout were introduced in 1883 to Michigan's Pere Marquette River. They proved much better adapted to the changing river conditions from logging and development than the brook trout that replaced the grayling. By around 1920, brown trout were the dominant trout species in the coldwater rivers and streams of the Upper Midwest. Browns did not respond well to the bright, gaudy patterns that brook trout anglers used. New fly patterns began to emerge focused on tricking wary browns. We will see this as we review patterns presented in this book.

Pacific salmon were planted in the Great Lakes during the 1970s to combat exploding populations of invasive alewives. This created a huge sportfishing boom that still continues today. There are naturalized populations of salmon across the lakes, although stocking still continues in many areas.

The abundant warmwater opportunities of the region were not overlooked by fly anglers. In 1881, Dr. James Henshall of Cincinnati, Ohio, published the *Book of the Black Bass*. A part of this book focused on fly-fishing techniques for bass, and Henshall created one of the first fly patterns designed specifically to target bass: the Henshall Bug. Interest in warmwater fly fishing became firmly established, as there were numerous close-to-home opportunities for many anglers. Fly fishing for bass, especially smallmouth, has increased significantly in recent decades.

Fly pattern development continued all through the 1900s and is still happening. The Upper Midwest has been a driving force, with many recognized "day-to-day" patterns and tying techniques coming from the region. In spite of all the advancements in tying and techniques, a number of these flies have stood the test of time and are still used in their original form.

Women also played a significant role. The fly-tying industry in the United States was started in Stevens Point, Wisconsin, by Carrie Frost. In 1919, Frost had over 150 area women tying flies for her. Also from Wisconsin, Helen Shaw wrote one of the earliest (1963), and probably still one of the best, beginner instructional fly-tying books, simply called *Fly Tying*. Michigan's Ann Schweigert is also credited for a number of fly creations

Various tying techniques were developed and refined in the Upper Midwest. William Avery Bush developed the parachute style of hackling a dry.

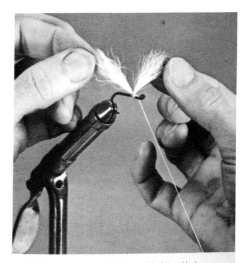

18h. Place one more turn of thread around the hair and hook immediately in front of the divided tuft and the wing is complete. The angle of the V between the wings can be adjusted by the angle at which you hold them as you circle each one with the tying thread. Practice this wing until you can divide it evenly and are able to set the two halves at the same angle each time. Crossing the thread between the tufts and circling each one with it will become a simple process once you have familiarized yourself with it through practice.

SINGLE WING—DRY FLY　　　　　　　　　169

The book Fly Tying, *featuring Helen Shaw as the tier, was the first to show photos of individual tying steps. Shaw was a well-known commercial tier from Sheboygan, Wisconsin. She is often referred to as "the First Lady of Fly Tying."*

Michigan's Au Sable River system played a significant role in fly pattern development through much of the twentieth century and beyond. The area served as a natural laboratory for guides and tiers to test and refine fly patterns. A number of today's most popular patterns got their start there.

Clarence Roberts and/or Earl Madsen first tied deer hair parallel to the hook shank to form a body. Madsen is also credited as being the first to use rubber strands as legs in a fly. Dan Gapen is credited with the spun deer hair head on a streamer, creating the Muddler Minnow. The late Chris Helm was perhaps the best deer hair artist ever.

Many notable fly tiers had or have roots in this area. Moving down the time line a short list can include names like Earl Madsen, Ernie Schwiebert, Doug Swisher and Carl Richards, Gary Borger, Larry Dahlberg, Kelly Galloup, Russ Maddin, Tommy Lynch, Kevin Feenstra, Ray Schmidt, and

a host of others I apologize for not naming here. The list could be long and extensive.

Perhaps the most difficult task in writing this book was trying to narrow it down to just fifty pattern designs. Due to the species diversity of the region, the significant contrast in types of water fished, and the various techniques employed, you'll see that the list has gone well beyond fifty. Even then, there are many more patterns that could have been included.

The final pattern selection was based on several factors. First, I tried to be representative of the various fisheries around the Upper Midwest. I contacted an assortment of top anglers and guides to get their input as to various important patterns. Finally, I also factored in my own five decades of fly-fishing experience across the region.

As you review the patterns, you'll see that some are quite old, while others are quite new. It seems we are presently in a renaissance of tying materials. The assortment of synthetic materials continues to grow, allowing a new era of creativity in fly design. The use of brushes has simplified the construction of complex streamer patterns. Hook designs have also advanced significantly, and there are more brands on the market than ever. The assortment of thread available for tying has also expanded, with stronger, thinner offerings available.

I've tried to present the most common recipe for each pattern. Where known, I have listed the originator of a specific pattern. The flies pictured are from different sources. Some are from the originator, some are from commercial sources, and I personally tied a number of them.

Every effort has been made to properly credit individuals for patterns they created. This was done through various avenues of research including previously published works, online sources, and discussion with tiers. Even so, this is not always 100 percent correct.

As we will see, there can be questions concerning even very notable designs. Both Al Caucci and Swisher and Richards were concurrently working to improve Fran Betters's Haystack pattern. Caucci was first to introduce the Comparadun name, but it may be that Swisher and Richards came up with the actual design first. We may never know for sure.

If there is disagreement on any pattern origination or creation as listed, please accept my sincere apologies. These were based on the best information I could find. I truly regret if any of this is in error.

Hook and material substitution is certainly allowed where applicable and is a part of the creative tying process. The appendix gives additional information that was not part of the main body. This is mainly the review of several multistep tying techniques that many readers may not be familiar with.

You may or may not agree with the list of patterns I have selected. If a certain tier or pattern was left out, it certainly was not a deliberate omission and, again, I apologize for this. What is presented here is a comprehensive assortment of significant patterns that can be used across the region. The flies given here are all proven fish catchers and have earned the right to be part of a fly selection for the waters of the Upper Midwest.

RESOURCES

Books

Darkes, Jerry. *Essential Flies for the Great Lakes Region*. Lanham, MD: Stackpole Books, 2020.

Greenburg, Josh. *Rivers of Sand*. Guilford, CT: Lyons Press, 2014.

Miller, Ann. *Pocket Guide to Upper Midwest Hatches*. Lanham, MD: Stackpole Books, 2023.

Websites

www.currentworks.com
www.mangledfly.com
www.schlutzoutfitters.com

YouTube

Mad River Outfitters
Schultz Outfitters
Tying Michigan's Best Trout Flies

TROUT ON TOP

The Hexagenia limbata *mayfly, known simply as "the Hex," is one of the most recognized insects for Upper Midwest fly anglers. The Hex hatch is a key seasonal event in the area and brings some of the largest fish to the surface to feed. Kevin Feenstra photo*

*T*he dry fly has reached much of its present state of development through the efforts of Upper Midwest anglers and tiers. Many of the patterns, current material applications, and tying techniques had their origins in this region. Various early designs were generalist or attractors. But as fish species changed and knowledge of the entomology of the area grew, specific imitations began to appear.

The mayfly (order Ephemeroptera) rules across the region as the most recognized and imitated insect. They are abundant in all moving waters as well as many lakes. A full range of species is represented here, from the tiny Trico to the giant Hex. The primary mayfly species are shown with various stages of development represented. This allows many options to create flies for "selective trout."

The various tiers show different paths to reach similar conclusions. Specific pattern templates are presented where by varying hook size and material coloration, a range of mayfly species can be imitated. Ed McCoy's duns and spinners represent the latest in materials and technique, while Jerry Regan's spinners give a link to the earlier designs from the region. This theme is repeated through the chapters.

Caddis (order Tricoptera) and stoneflies (order Plecoptera) are represented less. This is not to diminish their importance; they just do not share the same status as the mayfly in the region and their application is often more localized. Terrestrial patterns received their first specific recognition in this area. Night flies have turned into an art form all their own.

Finally, I want to emphasize again that I have tried to give all pattern recipes in their original form with as much detail as possible. Some of the descriptions are quite generic, so it will be up to the tier to select a usable item. Hook, thread, and material substitutions can be made if an item is not available. Let logic rule here—this is a part of the creative process of fly tying.

Left to right: Modern Adams, Flat-Wing Adams, Parachute Adams

Adams

It would be difficult to go fly fishing for trout anywhere in the world and open an angler's fly box without finding some version of an Adams dry fly. Few flies have the universal acceptance by both anglers and trout given to this venerable pattern. The Adams dry fly was created in 1922 by Michigan angler/tier Len Halladay in honor of his friend Dr. Charles Adams for use on the Boardman River near Traverse City. The pattern is reflective of the Catskill-style dries of the period and the original design is still catching fish today.

Over the years, the Adams dry has gone through several transformations. The spent wings evolved into upright. The water-absorbing wool body was replaced with muskrat underfur, then rabbit, and later synthetic materials. The pheasant tippet tail is now hackle fibers. The Barred Plymouth Rock hackle is now referred to simply as "grizzly" and the Rhode Island Red hackle as "brown."

The modern version given here is the most recognized recipe. It is a pattern that imitates nothing in particular, but has a live, buggy look to it that trout definitely like. The parachute version of this fly is often used during the *Callibaetis* mayfly hatch of western US stillwaters, so has inadvertently become a hatch-matcher pattern.

MODERN ADAMS
(Unknown)

- **Hook:** #10-20 standard dry fly
- **Thread:** Black or gray 8/0 UNI-Thread
- **Tail:** Grizzly and brown hackle fibers, mixed
- **Body:** Muskrat underfur or gray synthetic dry-fly dubbing
- **Wings:** Grizzly hackle tips, upright and divided
- **Hackle:** Grizzly and brown, mixed

Note: A well-marked cree hackle can be substituted for the mixed grizzly/brown and help simplify the tying process. These capes and saddles are hard to find and command a premium price, but save tying time.

The parachute version of the Adams (and all dry flies) is best on smooth water and flows. This design sits in the surface film, giving a realistic impression and likely taken as both duns and spinners on any given day. The fully hackled design floats better on rougher, more turbulent flows where a parachute would likely be sunk.

In my early days of tying, quality dry-fly hackle was hard to find and costly for a young tier. Metz, Hoffman, or Whiting hackle was not yet on the scene. No way was I going to sacrifice any valued grizzly hackle for wings. Mallard flank was plentiful and looked similar. There was a mixed-color hackle called "Variant" and I searched out those with the most brown fibers. Tied with a gray body this fly looked kind of like an Adams. Originally called the Half-Ass Adams, it is now just the Half Adams. It caught fish then, and still does today. It is not pictured, but you get the idea.

A down-wing version of the Adams is a great general caddis imitation. A variety of materials can be used for the wing such as deer or elk hair, calf tail, mink guard hairs, or similar stiff fibers. These can be fished on fast, turbulent flows. The version shown here I call the Flat-Wing Adams has hackle-tip wings and clipped hackle to sit flush on the surface as a spent caddis and is used on smooth flows. It may also be taken as a terrestrial or possibly even a spent or crippled mayfly.

The Adams can be tied smaller than a size 20, but at this point, I would forget about putting wings on. This process is just too difficult and time-consuming. A hackle-only version works well and catches fish. On smooth flows it sometimes helps to clip the hackle on the bottom.

All in all, we can call the Adams "the universal dry-fly pattern." If one were limited to fishing one single dry fly for trout anywhere, this would likely be the one. The combination of colors and materials is adaptable to the full range of dry-fly designs and an extensive variety of insects. I've taken credit for one of these variations with the disclaimer that I had not seen this done before I tied it.

PARACHUTE ADAMS
(Unknown)

- **Hook:** #10-20 standard dry fly
- **Thread:** Black or gray 8/0 UNI-Thread
- **Tail:** Grizzly and brown hackle fibers, mixed
- **Body:** Muskrat underfur or gray dry-fly dubbing
- **Wing:** Single upright post of bright calf tail, Hi-Viz, or similar material
- **Hackle:** Grizzly and brown, mixed

Note: When wrapping a parachute hackle, start up the post and make each wrap below the other to the top of the body. Also, try to wrap both hackles at the same time. This keeps the fibers much neater and saves a bit of time.

FLAT-WING ADAMS
(Jerry Darkes)

- **Hook:** #14-16 Daiichi 1180
- **Thread:** Gray 70D UTC
- **Body:** Gray dry-fly dubbing
- **Wings:** Grizzly hackle tips, tied flat alongside of body
- **Hackle:** Grizzly and brown, mixed, or cree, trimmed flat on bottom

Note: This can be tied in other sizes, but size 14 and 16 are what I normally use. If all else fails for rising fish, give it a try. If you substitute peacock herl for the body, you have a passable deer fly imitation.

HALLADAY ADAMS
(Len Halladay)

- **Hook:** #10-14 standard dry fly
- **Thread:** Black 6/0 Danville
- **Tail:** Golden pheasant tippet fibers
- **Body:** Gray wool dubbing
- **Wings:** Barred Plymouth Rock hackle tips, tied oversize and three-quarters spent
- **Hackle:** Barred Plymouth Rock and Rhode Island Red rooster hackle, tied oversize and full

Note: The original Halladay Adams has an understated beauty to it. Give it a try sometime. Catching a fish on one gives a satisfying link to the fly-fishing heritage of the region.

Halladay's original Adams design is now over a hundred years old. The wings were tied three-quarters spent, and the tail was golden pheasant tippet fibers. It will still catch trout today. Give it a try!

Top: Griffith's Gnat, two sizes; bottom, left to right: Indicator Gnat, Emerger Gnat

Griffith's Gnat

This pattern holds a significant spot in fly-fishing history, as it is named for Michigan fly angler George Griffith, the founding father of Trout Unlimited. Whether Griffith actually created this pattern is not known for sure. Famed rod builder Paul Young may have developed it and named it after Griffith, or another tier named Walt Shaw tied it first. What we know for sure is that this was one of the first patterns to address trout feeding on tiny insects generically referred to as "midges."

Griffith met fellow angler George Mason while fishing the Au Sable near Burton's Landing in the summer of 1950. Over several years they laid the groundwork of an organization focused on their shared interest of protecting trout and their habitat. On July 18, 1959, Griffith, Mason, and fourteen other concerned men met at Griffith's cabin on the Au Sable and formed the group now known as Trout Unlimited.

Griffith's Gnat is another universal pattern that has taken trout everywhere they are found. It doesn't imitate any specific insect or even family of insects, but is effective when various small chironomids and Diptera are active. It has a buggy, lifelike look to it and might be taken as a single insect or as a cluster of smaller insects. The combination of peacock herl and palmered grizzly hackle is undoubtedly attractive to trout.

There are several drawbacks to the pattern. It is best fished on calm, flat water but is still hard to see, especially in low light when midges are often actively hatching. There are several ways to address this. Where two flies can be fished at the same time, a larger, more visible fly is used with the Griffith's Gnat tied as a trailer 15 to 20 inches behind. If only a single fly is used, a bit of bright yarn can be tied in at the head of the fly to help track it on the water.

Also, the body and hackle are a bit fragile and may break and unwind after a few fish or when being removed from the fish. Counter-wrap through the body and hackle with extra-fine wire

Griffith's Gnat is another pattern with universal appeal to trout. Created on Michigan's Au Sable River system, it can be fished whenever fish are feeding on tiny insects. The mix of peacock herl and grizzly hackle gives a lifelike appearance on the water.

or fine (5X, 6X) tippet material. This will give extra strength to the fly and help hold it together.

A variation I have tied and fished for a number of years I call the Emerger Gnat or Half Gnat. It has produced well in a variety of locations when the regular Griffith's Gnat is not producing or may not be right for the situation. I usually tie the rear body in black or cream, but this can be changed as wanted. In this configuration I feel it can be taken as a wide range of smaller emerging insects including various mayflies and microcaddis.

As I've aged, this is a situation where using a short-shank, wide-gap hook for tying has helped. For example, a size 18 Daiichi 1310 has the shank length of a standard size 20 hook. The wider-gap hook is easier to remove and likely holds fish better. It makes it easier to unhook a fish, leading to an easier release and less chance of breaking off the fly.

GRIFFITH'S GNAT
(George Griffith)

- **Hook:** #16-24 standard dry fly
- **Thread:** Black 8/0 UNI-Thread
- **Body:** Peacock herl
- **Hackle:** Grizzly
- **Rib:** Extra-fine wire or 6X tippet, counter-wrapped over body and hackle

Note: As hook size decreases, going to a finer thread will reduce bulk. This is very helpful when working around the eye of the hook and tying the thread off. Veevus 10/0 has proven to be a great thread for use on flies size 20 and smaller.

INDICATOR GNAT
(Unknown)

- **Hook:** #16-24 Daiichi 1180
- **Thread:** Black 8/0 UNI-Thread
- **Body:** Peacock herl
- **Sighter/wing:** Orange or chartreuse Hi-Viz or McFly Foam
- **Hackle:** Grizzly
- **Rib:** Extra-fine wire or 6X tippet

Note: Trim the sighter material slightly longer than the hackle.

EMERGER GNAT
(Unknown)

- **Hook:** #16-24 standard dry fly
- **Thread:** Black or cream 70D UTC
- **Tail:** Clear Antron
- **Abdomen:** Tying thread
- **Thorax:** Peacock herl
- **Hackle:** Grizzly, can be trimmed flat on bottom if needed

Note: If fish are rising to midges and the standard Griffith's Gnat isn't working, give this a try. Black and cream are the two basic colors normally used, but you can substitute other thread colors as desired.

Top, left to right: Madsen's Dry Skunk, Modern Michigan Skunk; bottom: Improved Skunk

Michigan Skunk

While assembling the pattern list for this book, I surveyed a number of well-known anglers across the region. When I asked for top "must-have" trout patterns, the Skunk was on almost everyone's list. Despite being eighty years old, its popularity is a testament to the continued effectiveness of the fly. The Skunk also still holds a revered spot in fly bins across northern Michigan and beyond.

Also called Madsen's Skunk or the Au Sable Skunk, it was developed by Earl Madsen in the early 1940s. Madsen was a river guide from Grayling and a prolific commercial fly tier. Among other things, he may have been the first to incorporate rubber legs on flies. These are said to have come from the inner windings of golf balls or from automobile seats.

We would have to call the Skunk an attractor pattern, as it doesn't imitate anything specific, but has a lot of movement in the water. Perhaps the closest match would be an adult stonefly or a cricket. If the body is changed to yellow, it becomes a passable hopper pattern. Regardless, the pattern has a knack to move and attract fish.

The Skunk could be called a universal fly pattern, as there is also a wet version of it. As a dry, it can be used any time of the day in any type of weather. It can be dead-drifted, twitched, or popped and be effective. There really is not an incorrect way to fish the fly.

The original version had a body of black chenille and tail of gray squirrel. Early Michigan tiers only had materials that could be obtained easily or harvested locally, so game bird feathers, deer hair, and squirrel were commonly used. Much of this basic, "use what is at hand" tying philosophy has carried over to the present time in various patterns still coming out of the area.

If there is a weakness to the original Skunk design, it would be the deer hair wing. This can get damaged fairly quickly after a few fish. Currently

The introduction of brown trout displaced brook trout across much of the Upper Midwest. New fly designs were needed to consistently catch wary browns. Madsen's Skunk was an early pattern created to fool browns and is still a great fish producer today.

tied versions reinforce the deer hair with several wide X wraps and a bit of superglue or Zap-A-Gap.

You can replace the water-absorbing chenille body with poly yarn. A black or brown hackle can also be wrapped in front of the wing. This increases floatation and in larger sizes also turns it into a viable night fly, as it has a larger silhouette and pushes more water.

Ted Kraimer of Current Works Guide Service developed an updated version of the Skunk that addresses the weakness of the deer hair wing and adds even more additional floatation. He normally fishes this as a "twitch" fly with a bit of movement. It also dives when stripped sharply, opening up a whole other world of possibilities for this pattern.

MADSEN'S DRY SKUNK
(Earl Madsen)

- **Hook:** #8 Mustad 94840
- **Thread:** Black 3/0 Danville
- **Tail:** Gray squirrel tail
- **Body:** Black chenille
- **Wing:** Deer hair
- **Legs:** White rubber strands

Note: As productive of a trout fly as the Skunk is, it crosses over to the warmwater realm effectively.

The original black works well, but add a few other colors into the mix including yellow, olive, and even purple.

MODERN MICHIGAN SKUNK DRY
(Unknown)

- **Hook:** #8-12 standard dry fly
- **Thread:** Black 3/0 Danville
- **Tail:** White calf tail
- **Body:** Black poly yarn or dubbing, with one strand of rubber hackle on each side
- **Legs:** White rubber hackle
- **Wing:** Natural deer body hair to extend just past the tail, leaving the trimmed butt ends of the deer hair and covering with X wraps or hackle to help strengthen the wing
- **Hackle:** Black or brown, wrapped over the butt ends of the deer hair (optional)

Note: As mentioned in the intro to the pattern, this update also brings the Skunk into use as a night fly. It can also carry over as a warmwater pattern and be tied with different body and rubber hackle colors to create different looks.

IMPROVED SKUNK
(Ted Kraimer)

- **Hook:** #10 Gamakatsu S10
- **Thread:** Black 6/0 UNI-Thread
- **Tail:** White calf tail
- **Body:** Black UV Ice Dub, with a strip of black 2 mm foam tied in at back and pulled over top and secured
- **Underwing:** Pearl Krystal Flash
- **Wing:** Natural deer body hair
- **Head:** Remainder of black foam strip, pulled back over top, secured over wing, then trimmed
- **Legs:** Medium white round rubber hackle

Note: The use of updated materials really brings the Skunk into the modern fly-fishing era. This is a great facelift and also increases the durability significantly.

Borchers Drake, two sizes

Borchers Drake Parachute

In the history of trout fishing in America, the rivers of northern Michigan, especially the Au Sable and Manistee systems, are particularly noteworthy. After advancing beyond the Catskill area of New York State, this is where the next phase of trout-fishing development took place. Several decades after the sad demise of the Michigan grayling, the brown trout established itself as the dominant species.

Anglers had to develop patterns to fool the harder-to-catch browns. The gaudy attractor patterns that worked so well on the native brook trout gained little attention from the snooty European brown trout. More-realistic designs in natural colors began to appear from the vises of local tiers. This transition took place through the early part of the twentieth century.

Borchers Drake is fly pattern with a bit of confusion around it. It is a creation of Ernie Borcher, or is it Borchers? Some sources say the *s* is at the end of the last name, others say it is not. Then, what does it really represent? Some say a Brown Drake, others say the Mahogany (*Leptophlebia*) or Black Quill mayfly. Finally, some say the fly was actually the creation of Anne Schweigert of Luzerne, Michigan, and Borcher (or Borchers) added grizzly hackle and his name.

Regardless, this is a "gap fly," somewhat like the Adams, that shows the Catskill influence in its design, but toned down and more natural in appearance. Borchers Drake still holds a place of significance in the trout-rich regions of northern Michigan. In her very comprehensive *Pocket Guide to Upper Midwest Hatches*, Ann Miller lists Borchers Drake as an imitation of the Great Mahogany dun and spinner. As she is both an accomplished aquatic biologist and fly angler, we will go with Miller's classification.

Ultimately, Borchers Drake can be used during a number of the early mayfly hatches such as Hendricksons, March Browns, Mahoganies, Black Quills, and *Isonychia*, and oddly enough, it often produces well when Sulphurs are present. It is also a very usable pattern whenever brown-colored spinners are on the water.

As is often the case, the current version of the fly has changed noticeably from the original. The original body material, condor quill, is now illegal to possess. This has been replaced by mottled turkey quill fibers. Moose mane fibers are now used instead of pheasant tail fibers for the tail. While it can still be found tied with conventional-style hackle, the parachute version is almost exclusively used, as it is often fished when spinners are on the water.

The parachute version of the fly was first tied by Tim Neal in 1983, when he worked at the Fly Factory in Grayling, Michigan. According to Neal, he figured that since the original Borchers Drake was a good fly, the parachute would be even better. Even that design has changed a bit over time, as the brown hackle is often left out now and the hackle post can be replaced with a synthetic material. Neal

Borchers Drake has been a staple in northern Michigan fly shop bins for decades. This pattern can be fished whenever darker-colored mayflies are present. It can be tied from a size 12 down to a size 18.

has an interesting YouTube channel called "Tying Michigan's Best Trout Flies" that is well worth checking out.

BORCHERS DRAKE PARACHUTE
(Tim Neal)

- **Hook:** #12-16 standard dry fly
- **Thread:** Black 6/0 Danville
- **Tail:** Three moose mane fibers, tied long
- **Post:** Fine white deer belly hair
- **Body:** Mottled turkey tail quill fibers
- **Hackle:** Brown and grizzly

Roberts Yellow Drake, one heavily hackled and one sparsely hackled

Roberts Yellow Drake

As the trend in more-realistic fly designs continued, tying techniques evolved and additional patterns appeared on the scene. The Great Depression became a driving force for this along with the need for more improved designs to target wary brown trout. In the smooth flows of the northern Michigan rivers, the hackled designs of the Catskill dry-fly patterns were not the answer.

Detroit fly tier William Avery Bush developed the parachute style of hackling a fly. This allowed the fly to sit lower in the water with a more realistic profile. The hackle fibers still provided additional floatation. In 1934, Bush was awarded a patent for a hook with a metal post on it for wrapping hackle horizontally and parallel to the hook shank. He licensed the hooks to William Mills & Son, who created a series of patterns on them referred to as a "Gyrofly."

Clarence Roberts was a game warden from Grayling, Michigan, and his home water was the South Branch of the Au Sable River. His Yellow Drake from the 1950s is still catching trout today. It also has special historical fly-tying significance, as it combines both the parachute hackle and the parallel deer hair body. This is a pattern that has stood the test of time and is still found in fly shop bins across northern Michigan. It could be a staple in fly shops anywhere.

Roberts adapted Bush's parachute-style hackle to a standard hook by adding a winding post. It may be that these hooks were hard to get or just too expensive to use in quantity, so Roberts added the white deer hair post for the hackle. This allowed the fly to float low and present a realistic profile on the smooth flows of the Au Sable. The white post also increased visibility on the water. The amount of hackle used can be varied.

Both Clarence Roberts and Earl Madsen are credited with popularizing the deer hair body tied parallel to and around the hook shank. There is disagreement as to who first did this. Both men were products of the 1930s Depression. With tying materials and cash scarce, fly tiers used materials that were readily available, and Michigan did have plenty of whitetail deer. Not having the luxury of today's high-tech floatants, it was also a buoyant as well as durable body when tied correctly.

This original coloration mimics light-colored mayflies from the giant *Hexagenia* to various Sulphur species just by changing hook sizes. In his book *Rivers of Sand*, Josh Greenburg says of Roberts Drake, "If you tie it in a #16, it works for the Sulphurs. A #14 is a can't miss March Brown. In a #10, is a perfect Brown Drake and a #6 is just fine for the Hex."

After the publication of Carl Swisher and Doug Richards's groundbreaking *Selective Trout* in 1971, more emphasis was placed on creation of patterns that matched specific mayfly species. Much of Swisher and Richards's work had been done right on the Au Sable River itself, so their patterns gained favor over many older, classic designs. In spite of this, Roberts Yellow Drake continued to hold a spot in fly bins as it continued to catch fish.

The basic template of this pattern is adaptable to a wide range of mayfly species. By altering thread

Roberts Yellow Drake was one of the earliest parachute-style patterns and one of the first to tie deer hair parallel to the hook shank for the body. Tied with yellow thread it mimics a variety of light-colored mayflies. By substituting different colors of thread in place of the original yellow, a variety of color schemes are created that can be used to imitate different mayflies.

color and hook size, a multitude of color schemes can be created and a full range of mayflies imitated. As we'll see later with Rusty's Spinner, you can change the deer body hair color, too. Roberts Yellow Drake is worthy of a spot in fly boxes everywhere. Give it a try no matter where you fish.

ROBERTS YELLOW DRAKE
(Clarence Roberts)

- **Hook:** #8-16 Mustad 94831
- **Thread:** Yellow 6/0 Danville
- **Tail:** Pheasant tail fibers
- **Body:** Natural deer hair
- **Wing post:** White deer belly hair
- **Hackle:** Ginger

Note: The significance of this fly can't be overstated. From the parachute post and hackling style to the deer hair body, it can be fished on smooth water worldwide. Whenever light-colored mayflies are on the water, a correctly sized Roberts Yellow Drake will likely catch trout.

Top: Sulphur Dun Parachute; bottom, left to right: Male Hendrickson Parachute, Female Hendrickson Parachute

Parachutes You Need

For many anglers the appearance of the *Ephemerella subvaria* mayfly, aka Hendrickson, signifies the real "start" of the trout season, as it is the first to get good numbers of fish looking up and provide consistent dry-fly action. It is the major early-season mayfly hatch on most waters east of the Mississippi.

The hatch timing can vary considerably depending on latitude. On places like Ohio's Mad River, Hendricksons often start in March, while in northern Michigan and Wisconsin and southern Ontario, they may not show until late May.

Males and females differ in both color and size, so both patterns are presented here. Trout will often show preference for one or the other on a given day, so it pays to carry both. If regulations permit, it is possible to fish them together rigged in tandem to see if there is a preference.

Hendricksons often hatch in inclement weather. It isn't unusual for them to appear during a spring snow squall. Full development and emergence are slowed down when it is cold. Trout have ample time to selectively feed on duns and emergers, and again may show preference for one stage over another. We'll also review Hendrickson emerger patterns.

The Hendrickson emergence can last for several weeks with duns appearing in the early afternoon,

A male Hendrickson dun mayfly, Ephemerella subvaria. *The male is smaller than the female and has a pinkish-brown body color. It is considered the first "big hatch" of the season and the start of dry-fly activity. Cold temperatures can keep duns on the water a long time after they hatch, giving trout plenty of time to feed on them. Ann Miller photo*

then showing later in the day as the weather continues to warm. Spinners will appear within two days of hatching, generally over riffle areas in early evening.

The color selectivity trout often have for the male or female Hendrickson was highlighted a long time ago in *Art Flick's Streamside Guide*, published in 1947. Here the recipe for the early Catskill-style female pattern listed a body made from "the urine-stained underbelly fur of a female fox" to get the pink coloration needed. Fortunately, today's tier has multiple natural and synthetic dubbing options available.

Flick also lamented the lack of good dun hackle to tie the Hendrickson and other patterns to match important mayflies. Again, the modern fly tier has multiple sources of high-quality dun-colored dry-fly hackle. Sourcing the materials is no longer a problem.

As noted in the previous chapter, the parachute-hackling style is well suited to the smooth flows found across the Upper Midwest. It also presents a realistic profile of most mayfly species. When hackling a parachute pattern, we can also go slightly larger with the hackle. Instead of using a hackle length of one and half times the hook gap, we should go closer to two times the hook gap.

By making minor adjustments, this pattern template easily imitates a number of mayflies. For example, if you drop the hook size to 16 and use a yellow dubbing, we have an excellent imitation of the Sulphur Dun of the Midwest and Pale Morning Dun of the western US. We will take a closer look at the Sulphur Dun in the next chapter.

HENDRICKSON PARACHUTE
(Unknown)

- **Hook:** #14 standard dry fly
- **Thread:** Tan (for the female) or brown (for the male) 8/0 UNI-Thread
- **Wing post:** Dun or gray Antron, Z-Lon, or similar synthetic material
- **Tail:** Dun hackle fibers or Microfibetts
- **Body:** Female: pinkish-tan synthetic or fur dubbing, commercially called Hendrickson Pink; male: tan synthetic or fur dubbing
- **Hackle:** Blue dun

SULPHUR DUN PARACHUTE
(Unknown)

- **Hook:** #16-18 standard dry fly
- **Thread:** Yellow 8/0 UNI-Thread
- **Wing post:** Dun or gray Antron, Z-Lon, or similar synthetic material
- **Tail:** Dun hackle fibers
- **Body:** Yellow dry-fly dubbing
- **Hackle:** Blue dun

Left to right: Sulphur Sparkle Dun, Sulphur Dun Comparadun, Female Hendrickson Biot Comparadun, Lighthouse Slate Wing Olive, Lighthouse Hendrickson Dun. (See Appendix B on p. 131 for recipes for the two Lighthouse flies.)

Companion Comparaduns

The Comparadun style of fly goes back to the 1960s and is credited to Al Caucci, who fished the Catskill area and Delaware River in New York. It is considered an improvement on Fran Betters's original Haystack pattern. Caucci teamed with Bob Nastasi and published a book called *Hatches* in the early 1970s, where the Comparadun was introduced to the fly-fishing world.

This is surrounded by controversy, as during the same time period, Doug Swisher and Carl Richards were working on Michigan's Au Sable River and expanding the use of specific insect-imitating dry flies. Their *Selective Trout* was published in 1972 and showed a pattern called the Hairwing No-Hackle, also an advancement from Betters's Haystack. Regardless, both books were groundbreaking works and helped set the stage for dry-fly fishing as it is practiced today.

The Comparadun is another pattern template that can be easily adjusted to imitate a wide range of mayflies. Only three materials are required, and it is quite easy to tie. Having the right deer hair for the wing is the key to the pattern. It has to be short and fine, especially for smaller sizes.

Another version of the pattern showing its adaptability is the Sparkle Dun. This variation was developed by Craig Mathews of Blue Ribbon Flies in Montana. Here the tail fibers are replaced with a bit of brown or amber Sparkle Yarn or Z-Lon to imitate a mayfly emerging from the nymphal shuck. Locally, Mathews promoted this for the PMD, or Pale Morning Dun, hatch, which is essentially the western version of the Sulphur Dun. Coloration is nearly identical.

The Comparadun-style fly is well suited to the Sulphur Dun and Blue-Winged Olive hatches of the Upper Midwest. The Sulphur Dun is one of the most widespread and longest-lasting hatches across the region. It actually covers two distinct species: *Ephemerella invaria* is referred to as the

Sulphur Dun, Pale Evening Dun, and Light Hendrickson; *Epehemerella dorthea* is the Little Sulphur Dun. Size varies between them, and there are local color variations.

There are a number of *Baetis* mayfly species across the region called Blue-Winged Olives or Slate-Winged Olives. The largest of these are a size 14 and they range down to a size 22. Though small in size, they often hatch in abundance and can produce multiple broods per season.

The *Baetis* genus includes several species and represents the first mayfly to hatch as well as one of the last. In between they can appear most anytime, generally during the coolest periods of the day. *Baetis* also hatch during cool to cold weather in a light rain or even snow, so it can pay to sit streamside and observe during inclement conditions.

Blue-Winged Olives as well as Sulphurs are important mayflies of the Driftless area of Wisconsin, Minnesota, Iowa, and Illinois. Look where these four states come together, and this is the Driftless—a unique area of glacial drift, with numerous limestone-based spring creeks. It is an isolated oasis of cold water in an otherwise warmwater area. There are hundreds of miles of trout water, much of which flows through public land. This area continues to gain popularity with anglers, as it is very reachable from several prominent urban areas.

Dennis Potter is a well-known figure among Midwest fly tiers and anglers. He operates Riverhouse Fly Company and offers a wide range of productive, self-designed fly patterns, along with instructional videos. His Lighthouse series of flies gives a unique variation of the original Comparadun design. These patterns sit low in the water and so are well suited to the smooth flow found across the region. The incorporation of the EP Fiber fluorescent indicator is a great help in tracking these flies on the water.

SULPHUR SPARKLE DUN
(Craig Mathews)

- **Hook:** #14-18 standard dry fly
- **Thread:** Yellow 8/0 UNI-Thread
- **Wing:** Fine bleached deer body hair
- **Shuck:** Amber or brown Sparkle Yarn or Z-Lon
- **Body:** Pale yellow poly or fur dubbing

Note: The trailing nymph shuck represented here can also be applied to a full range of mayfly and caddis patterns to imitate an emerging adult.

SULPHUR DUN COMPARADUN
(Al Caucci / Swisher and Richards)
- **Hook:** #14-18 standard dry fly
- **Thread:** Yellow 8/0 UNI-Thread
- **Wing:** Fine bleached deer body hair, set upright
- **Tail:** Dun hackle fibers or Microfibetts
- **Body:** Pale yellow poly or fur dubbing

Note: *Ephemerella invaria* can have a bit of an orange tint at times, so tie a few with burnt orange thread when dubbing the body. Tie the same fly in size 14, but change the body to Hendrickson Pink dubbing for a great Hendrickson imitation.

LT HENDRICKSON BIOT COMPARADUN
(Al Caucci and Bob Nastasi)

- **Hook:** #14 Daiichi 1100
- **Thread:** Tan 8/0 UNI-Thread
- **Tail:** Dun hackle fibers or Microfibetts
- **Abdomen:** Pink turkey biot
- **Thorax:** Tan or Hendrickson Pink dry-fly dubbing
- **Wing:** Fine deer hair

Top, left to right, McCoy All Day Duns: Hex, Iso, Brown Drake; bottom, McCoy Boondoggle Spinners: Hex, Iso, Brown Drake. (See Appendix B on pp. 131–32 for recipes for the McCoy Boondoggle Spinners flies.)

McCoy Mayflies

Ed McCoy is a very respected guide and gifted, innovative fly tier from northern Michigan. He holds degrees in zoology and in fisheries and wildlife from Michigan State University. His fly designs are cutting edge and have been featured in various national publications.

The All Day Dun and Boondoggle Spinner patterns presented here are great fish catchers and combine traditional materials and styles in an updated package. The use of foam for the body makes the fly super durable and virtually unsinkable—necessary attributes for a large mayfly pattern that allow for continuous, "All Day" use. The use of markers to complete the body brings an additional aspect of imitation rarely (if ever) seen on dry flies before. A

search on YouTube for "Ed McCoy All Day Dun" will bring several results with videos of him showing how to easily create these foam bodies.

For a trout angler, the Upper Midwest offers multiple opportunities to catch big brown trout on dry flies. The emergence of the big mayflies certainly fits the bill for this. Two of these, the Brown Drake (*Ephemera simulans*) and Hex (*Hexagenia limbata*) are burrowing mayflies found in lakes as well as numerous streams across the region. Crossing over into a warmwater environment in lakes, they are eaten eagerly by smallmouth bass, panfish, and even walleye.

Both of these big mayflies are eagerly anticipated by anglers. Brown Drakes are found in sandy and

Ed McCoy's foam mayflies are a cutting-edge design that blends old techniques with modern materials. These patterns, which imitate some of the largest mayfly species like the Hex and Brown Drake, will bring oversize browns to the surface to feed. This is often an after-dark event. Phil Cook photo

fine gravel bottoms. They can start to appear in late May, but most emerge in early June across the region. Look for them in the late afternoon and early evening. The hatch is condensed into a fairly short time frame, usually under three weeks. Once it gets started, duns and spinners are often on the water at the same time.

The Hex emergence is considered the peak of summer dry-fly fishing. Hex mayflies are found in a silty bottom and appear more in mid-June into July. Most of this is night fishing, with anglers staking out a pre-scouted spot and waiting for the bugs to (hopefully) appear after dark. For those who don't care to fish at night, using a Hex dry pattern from dawn until the sun is on the water can still produce fish on station from the night before.

There is a second Hex species worth mention. The *Hexagenia atrocaudata*, or Red Hex, emerges from mid-August into September and is more locally important. Substituting reddish-brown or claret thread for yellow on a size 8 Roberts Yellow Drake imitates this mayfly well.

Isonychia mayflies also go by the names of White-Gloved Howdy, Leadwing Coachman, Slate Drake, and Mahogany Drake. They are found in fast flows

around big rocks, usually on the edge of the strongest current. Iso mayflies hatch sporadically through the season, never in large numbers, but trout seem to relish them. There are several *Isonychia* species and as the season progresses the size diminishes a bit.

I've grouped these three mayflies together due to their size. There is certainly no shortage of effective patterns that imitate them, and it was a difficult decision to overlook a number of these to feature this design. Forgive me if I bypassed the one you think best. I hope you'll understand my reasoning.

MCCOY ALL DAY DUN— BROWN DRAKE
(Ed McCoy)

- **Hook:** #12-14 Gamakatsu B10S
- **Thread:** Rusty brown 6/0 UNI-Thread
- **Tail:** Moose body hair
- **Body:** Cream 2 mm sheet foam, colored with Prismacolor canary yellow and dark brown on top
- **Hackle:** One cree and one grizzly dyed golden straw
- **Wing:** Whitetail deer belly hair

MCCOY ALL DAY DUN—HEX
(Ed McCoy)

- **Hook:** #8 Gamakatsu B10S Stinger
- **Thread:** Yellow 6/0 UNI-Thread
- **Tail:** Moose body hair
- **Body:** Cream 2 mm sheet foam, colored with Prismacolor canary yellow with dark brown on top
- **Hackle:** One cree and one grizzly dyed golden straw
- **Wing:** Whitetail deer belly hair

MCCOY ALL DAY DUN—*ISONYCHIA*
(Ed McCoy)

- **Hook:** #10-14 Gamakatsu B10S Stinger
- **Thread:** Insect green 3/0 Danville
- **Tail:** Moose body hair
- **Body:** Gray 2 mm sheet foam, colored with Prismacolor warm grey on top
- **Hackle:** Two gray or dark dun dyed grizzly

Left to right: Dust Bunny—Isonychia, *Dust Bunny*—Hendrickson, *Dust Bunny Variant*—Sulphur

Dust Bunny

The Dust Bunny is an offshoot of the Usual, a pattern developed in upstate New York's Adirondack region by legendary fly tier Fran Betters. Quite simple, the Usual is tied with only one material. Natural snowshoe rabbit foot underfur is used for the body and the guard hairs for the tail and wing. The natural water repellency of the rabbit helped the fly to float extremely well, making it well suited to the fast flows and pocketwater of the Ausable River (not to be confused with Michigan's Au Sable River).

This now-classic pattern dates back around seventy years. The story is that Betters was looking at the hind foot of a snowshoe hare left from a hunting trip, trying to see if it had any use for fly tying. The hair on the footpad was unique—wiry and translucent. The underfur, also translucent, was easy to dub. Betters used this material as a replacement on his Haystack design. The result was an immediate success—it floated like a cork and caught fish.

The success of this pattern did not go unnoticed. Talk of Betters's new pattern slowly spread, and it was found to catch fish pretty much wherever it was used. The Upper Midwest region, particularly the northern parts of Michigan, Minnesota, and Wisconsin, is another area where snowshoe rabbits are found. With material sourced from a local game animal, the Usual became a familiar fly across the region.

This coincided with increased awareness of the various stages of stream insect emergence and the need to imitate these stages as presented by Swisher and Richards in *Selective Trout*. We know that much of the on-water work for the book took place on Michigan's Au Sable River. While the Usual did take fish on the Au Sable, results were inconsistent.

Fran Betters's Usual was the predecessor to the Dust Bunny series. The Usual was a general-use emerger pattern. The snowshoe hare material is high floating with a lifelike translucent appearance on the water. Rusty Gates turned it into an effective species-specific emerger imitation.

A bit more was needed for use on the glassy flows and snooty brown trout of the river.

Rusty Gates of Gates Lodge on the Au Sable took the Usual to the next level. Gates passed away in 2009 and is an iconic figure in the fly-fishing world. He was a tireless conservationist and worked constantly to protect and preserve the trout and wildlife of the Au Sable watershed, gaining numerous awards for his efforts.

Gates was also a gifted fly tier. By the age of seventeen he was tying flies commercially and guiding for the lodge, then owned by his parents. Gates was an observant student of the river as well as a meticulous tier. His book, *Seasons on the Au Sable*, was published in 2007 and chronicles a year on the river. In typical Rusty Gates fashion, all profits went to the Anglers of the Au Sable conservation group.

Gates developed a number of patterns now considered "must-haves" for fishing the area and is credited with the creation of the Dust Bunny. The Usual was considered an attractor pattern. Recognizing its characteristics as an emerger imitation, Gates adjusted materials to imitate specific mayflies. It is well suited for use wherever these insects are found. Josh Greenberg worked for Gates and took over the lodge after his death. According to

Greenburg, "the Dust Bunny is the ugliest fly we sell, but is the best Iso emerger I've fished."

DUST BUNNY—HENDRICKSON
(Rusty Gates)

- **Hook:** #12-14 TMC 100
- **Thread:** Burnt orange 6/0 UNI-Thread
- **Tail:** Dun snowshoe rabbit foot guard hair
- **Body:** Snowshoe rabbit foot underfur cut with Hendrickson Pink dubbing
- **Wing:** Dun snowshoe rabbit foot guard hair

DUST BUNNY VARIANT—SULPHUR
(Rusty Gates)

- **Hook:** #14-16 TMC 100
- **Thread:** Pale yellow 8/0 UNI-Thread
- **Tail:** Four or five wood duck fibers
- **Abdomen:** Yellow turkey biot
- **Thorax:** Yellow dry-fly dubbing
- **Wing:** Dun snowshoe rabbit foot guard hair

Note: This pattern imitates the almost-hatched dun. It goes a step beyond the true emerger, as the wing is upright and the body is almost fully out of the shuck.

DUST BUNNY—*ISONYCHIA*
(Rusty Gates)

- **Hook:** #12 Daiichi 1180
- **Thread:** Brown 8/0 UNI-Thread
- **Tail:** Dun snowshoe rabbit foot guard hair
- **Body:** Mix of one-third each brown olive SLF, gray SLF, and gray beaver dubbing
- **Wing:** Dun snowshoe rabbit foot guard hair, tied in a 45-degree V

Note: This was the original Dust Bunny color developed by Rusty Gates. The recipe given here is specific for the *Isonychia* emerger. The easiest way to blend the dubbing is a quick spin in a coffee grinder.

Top: Rusty's Spinner variation with Hi-Viz wings; bottom: Rusty's Spinner, two sizes

Rusty's Spinner

Calvin "Rusty" Gates is a memorable and historic figure in Midwest trout fishing. He ran Gates Au Sable Lodge in Grayling, Michigan, for a number of decades and is also remembered as a great tier and conservationist. Few people had the impact on trout fishing in the Upper Midwest that Gates did.

Gates is credited with a host of unique fly patterns he created for area waters. Some of these have a universal appeal on trout waters anywhere. Rusty's Spinner is at the top of the list. This is not to be confused with the generic Rusty Spinner pattern.

As with mayfly dun patterns, spinners are a needed component when fishing hatches. In the final stage of their life after mating, many mayflies drop and lay spent on the water, wings outstretched. This normally happens in the evening and also after dark, depending on species and weather conditions. At this point they are easy prey for feeding fish.

Spinner imitations are designed to match size, color, and floating profile. They are generally tied without hackle to lie flush in the surface film. Many mayflies turn rusty brown in the spinner phase, regardless of the body color of the dun.

This Isonychia *spinner shows the rusty-brown body color common to a number of mayfly species spinners. Rusty's Spinner imitates these insects well. Kevin Feenstra photo*

The generic Rusty Spinner pattern is most commonly used. It is a great fish-catching pattern, but has its drawbacks. It works well on smooth flows, but lacking any hackle, in faster, choppy runs the fly can get pulled under. It also becomes very difficult to see in low light.

Rusty's Spinner incorporates several distinctive tying characteristics of the region to address these deficiencies. The deer hair body tied parallel to the hook and the mixed grizzly/brown hackle with grizzly tips are northern Michigan developments. These help the buoyancy of the fly in a full range of flow situations.

Being fully hackled may seem to go against conventional thinking for a spinner pattern, but this gives the fly a versatility most spinner designs lack. It can easily be adjusted for the type of water being fished. On fast flows, keep it hackled. On flat water, trim the hackle flat on the bottom and top. It also imitates spinners at a point just before they hit the water or when they are bouncing as they drop eggs.

Other winging materials like Hi-Viz or Z-Lon can be substituted for the grizzly hackle tips. Don't be afraid to experiment and tie this pattern up several ways. On a given day, one variation may work better than another.

Rusty's Spinner is a true Upper Midwest fly pattern with far-reaching effectiveness. Though not well known out of the area, it can be fished whenever and wherever rusty-brown mayfly spinners are on the water. In the primary sizes, 12 through 18, this is a pattern to have in your trout fly box all the time, wherever you are trout fishing.

RUSTY'S SPINNER
(Rusty Gates)

- **Hook:** #6-18 standard dry fly
- **Thread:** Rusty brown 8/0 UNI-Thread
- **Tail:** Three moose fibers
- **Body:** Reddish-brown deer hair parallel to hook shank
- **Wings:** Grizzly hackle tips, tied three-fourths spent
- **Hackle:** Grizzly and brown, mixed

Top, left to right: Riverhouse Hendrickson Spinner, Simple Spinner—Ephoron; bottom: Simple Spinner—Sulphur, Simple Spinner—Trico, Simple Spinner—Little Sulphur

The clear flat wings of a spent mayfly spinner are easily imitated by the Simple Spinner design. By varying body size and color, nearly all mayfly speci of importance to Upper Midwest fly fishers can be imitated. This pattern is best on smooth flows. Kevin Feenstra photo

Simple Spinner

Spinners are the final life stage of the mayfly. After mating, females drop to the water, release their eggs, and then die. Males also die after mating and fall to the surface. Called a "spinner fall" when this happens, large numbers of dead and dying mayflies can be present that bring trout to the surface to feed. Having an accurate imitation of the insect on the water is critical to success.

This pattern template is likely the one most commonly used as a mayfly spinner imitation. There are numerous variations of this design, but the main components are basically the same: several tail fibers, sometimes tied in a split V; a thin abdomen; a heavier thorax where the wings come out perpendicular to the hook shank; and tied to lay fully spent or flat on the water.

Hackle fibers or synthetic Microfibetts are used for the tail. A number of materials including tying thread, thin fine-texture dubbing, or turkey biots make up the abdomen. The thorax is a heavier area of fine-texture dubbing, and the wings can be a synthetic such as Hi-Viz, Z-Lon, or poly yarn. Natural materials like CDC, hackle fibers, or hen hackle tips can also be used for the wings.

The hook size and material colors are selected to match the natural insect being imitated. Here we are looking at several specific species patterns usable across the region. Keep in mind that adjustments can be made as needed no matter where you are. In some cases, the addition of an egg sac made from yellow dubbing or egg yarn can enhance effectiveness. This is true mainly with Hendrickson and Sulphur spinners.

Spinner falls usually occur in the evening as daylight fades and also after dark. Trying to track your fly in low light when there are numerous naturals on the water can be a daunting task. A spinner pattern can be tied to increase visibility in low light. The Riverhouse Hendrickson addresses this with a post of fluorescent yellow yarn as well as adding an egg sac. The yellow post is most visible in fading light. In daylight, a fluorescent pink post is more visible and will aid in spotting a small spinner such as a Trico.

The *Ephoron* mayfly is a night emergence and spinner fall. I've included it because it is unique in that both duns and spinners are on the water at the same. Also called the White Fly, this hatch crosses over to warmer rivers that hold smallmouth bass, who feed heavily on this bug. Few smallmouth anglers stay long enough in the evening to see if it happens on their favorite river.

This pattern style is best suited for imitations of size 10 or smaller. Floatation can be a problem on larger patterns, and we will see several different designs that work better for the larger flies and faster flows. The Simple Spinner template presented here is relatively easy to tie with a minimum of materials needed. It is time-tested and catches fish.

SIMPLE SPINNER—*EPHORON*

(Unknown)

- **Hook:** #10 Daiichi 1280
- **Thread:** White 70D UTC
- **Tail:** Clear Microfibetts, tied split
- **Abdomen:** Tying thread or thin white dry-fly dubbing
- **Thorax:** White dry-fly dubbing
- **Wings:** White poly yarn

SIMPLE SPINNER—SULPHUR

(Unknown)

- **Hook:** #14-18 Daiichi 1100
- **Thread:** Pale yellow 8/0 UNI-Thread
- **Tail:** Dun hackle fibers or Microfibetts
- **Abdomen:** Tying thread or pale yellow dry-fly dubbing, kept thin
- **Thorax:** Pale yellow dry-fly dubbing
- **Wings:** Clear (white) Hi-Viz or similar synthetic

Note: The size 14 hook is specific for the *Ephemerella invaria*. The 16 and 18 cover the *Ephemerella dorthea*.

RIVERHOUSE HENDRICKSON SPINNER

(Dennis Potter)

- **Hook:** #14 TMC 100
- **Thread:** Brown 70D UTC
- **Tail:** Light dun Microfibetts, tied long
- **Egg sac:** Yellow Superfine Dubbing, in a ball
- **Body:** Tying thread
- **Thorax:** Brown Superfine Dubbing
- **Wings:** Clear crinkled Z-Lon
- **Post:** Fluorescent yellow yarn

SIMPLE SPINNER—TRICO

(Unknown)

- **Hook:** #22-24 Daiichi 1110 (see note below)
- **Thread:** Black 70D UTC
- **Tail:** Clear Microfibetts
- **Abdomen:** Tying thread
- **Thorax:** Black Superfine Dubbing
- **Wing:** Clear Hi-Viz or white poly yarn
- **Post:** Pink yarn

Note: Unhooking a fish caught on a small hook can be a difficult process. Using a 1X short hook a size larger (for example, the Daiichi 1310) gives a much wider hook gap with a similar shank length. Removing the hook is usually both quicker and easier, minimizing stress to the fish. The larger-gap hook also holds fish better.

Top, left to right: Bat Fly, Hex Spinner;
bottom: Gray Drake Spinner, Brown Drake Spinner

BAT FLY
(Jerry Regan)

- **Hook:** #14 Mustad 94840
- **Thread:** Gray 6/0 Danville
- **Tail:** Dun hackle fibers
- **Body:** Deer hair, tied parallel to hook shank. Set butt ends up at 90 degrees and wrap base with thread to make parachute post.
- **Wings:** Dun hen, tied spent
- **Hackle:** Dun, wound parachute style above wings

Regan Spinners

Jerry Regan provides a direct link between the early days of fly development on Michigan's Au Sable River and today. At nearly eighty years old, he still ties commercially for several shops in the Grayling area. Regan admits that his spinner patterns lack the "fly bin appeal" of more sophisticated, modern designs, but are often the "last resort" that will trick a stubborn brown that has refused everything else.

Regan developed a unique hackling style for his spinners that allows the wings to sit flush on the surface, but still provide good floatation on faster flows. This technique also adds visibility to the fly on the water in low-light conditions. These patterns were developed through the 1980s and have been catching fish ever since.

This design template can be used for mayflies anywhere. This book is not meant to be an instructional manual, but since few people know the tying procedure, the tying steps are shown with photographs in the appendix. Regan has a full series of mayfly imitations, but here we will look at several representative examples. Please note that the recipes given are Regan's originals, but the tier can update hook and thread per today's availability as desired.

The Bat Fly imitates several different *Baetisca* mayfly species. Though not well known, it is likely quite widespread. It hatches mainly at night and often overlaps with larger mayflies like *Isonychia* and *Hexagenia*. Despite being smaller in size, trout will often target *Baetisca* and ignore the larger insects. The Bat Fly is also a good pattern to fish during the day when the Hex hatch is on.

Like the Brown Drake and Hex duns, spinner patterns of the same species are important across the region, as they often bring the largest fish to

Regan Spinners will produce trout everywhere. Match body size and the tying thread to the size and color of the mayfly being imitated. The wing post gives added visibility on the water.

feed on the surface. Brown Drake spinners are two-toned in color, brown over yellow. They usually drop in massive clouds when conditions are right and can provide a memorable angling experience. However, they are unpredictable and while many might be seen in the air above the trees, nuances in the weather can keep them from dropping.

Fishing Hex spinners is a highly anticipated, after-dark adventure from a preselected stationary location. Feeding fish are located by sound. The fly is cast upstream toward the noise and the hook set if the fish rises again. Encountering a large fish after dark is a memorable experience. The Hex spinner fall is subject to the same weather influences as the Brown Drake.

Three different species of *Siphlonurus* mayflies are referred to as Gray Drakes, and they hatch in sequence from mid-May into July. The spinners receive all the attention, as duns are rarely ever available to anglers. The nymphs crawl out of the water onto aquatic vegetation, where they emerge. Groups of spinners gather at dusk and descend to the water as light fades, so fishing for them is also a nighttime undertaking.

Gray Drakes are found across the Upper Midwest, but abundance is much more localized than other large mayflies. Where plentiful, large mating clouds can form and when they drop, trout eagerly feed on them. Look for them over rapids and riffle areas.

Note: Be sure to keep the body short and fat and the wings long to properly tie this pattern!

BROWN DRAKE SPINNER

(Jerry Regan)

- **Hook:** #10 Mustad 9672
- **Thread:** Dark brown 3/0 Danville
- **Tail:** Pheasant tail fibers
- **Body:** Yellow poly yarn, deer hair parallel to hook shank over top
- **Wings:** Dun hen
- **Hackle:** Brown, wound parachute style above wings

HEX SPINNER

(Jerry Regan)

- **Hook:** #6 Mustad 9672
- **Thread:** Yellow 3/0 Danville
- **Tail:** Pheasant tail fibers
- **Body:** Deer hair, tied parallel to hook shank. Set butt ends up at 90 degrees and wrap base with thread to make parachute post.
- **Wings:** Grizzly or dun hen, tied spent
- **Hackle:** Brown, wound parachute style above wings

GRAY DRAKE SPINNER

(Jerry Regan)

- **Hook:** #10 Mustad 9672
- **Thread:** Green 3/0 Danville
- **Tail:** Three black moose body hairs
- **Body:** Dun deer hair
- **Wings:** Dun hen
- **Hackle:** Yellow grizzly and grizzly, mixed, wound parachute style above wings

Top: Grannom X-Caddis, Grannom with Egg Sac; middle: Olive X-Caddis; bottom: Craig's Spring Creek Caddis, two colors

Caddis Variants

The lack of caddis dry patterns from the Upper Midwest doesn't diminish their importance to anglers. Unfortunately, they just don't share the same status as the mayfly across the region. This likely follows the precedent set in the Catskills and Poconos during the early development of fly fishing in America, where the mayfly received the most recognition.

Caddis go through what is called a complete metamorphosis with three complete life stages: larva, pupa, and adult. All three stages provide the angler opportunity. The larvae are wormlike, some being free-living while others build shelters. The pupae may swim to the surface or crawl to the shore. Caddis adults are mothlike in appearance, with a wing that folds down over the back. All stages lack a tail.

While caddis are certainly abundant on most waters, we rarely encounter adults in a large size and abundance like the *Hexagenia* mayfly. There are some exceptions to this such as the sizable October Caddis, but it is not an abundant insect in the area and is also a night emerger. We find that Upper Midwest caddis patterns tend to be more generalist rather than specific imitations, although I'll go against this claim with the first pattern listed.

The patterns given here reflect the emerging pupa as it transitions to the adult. This is often the most vulnerable stage of development and provides the longest time of exposure to feeding trout. The

This springtime rainbow took an Opal X-Caddis. When there is a heavy caddis emergence, patterns with a trailing shuck are often more productive. It may be that the natural insects are easiest for trout to catch at this stage and are specifically targeted.

The Grannom is likely the most recognized caddis species of the Upper Midwest. It is widespread across the region and can overlap with the Hendrickson mayfly hatch. Kevin Feenstra photo

X-Caddis, a pattern of western origin, imitates this stage extremely well. Craig Mathews of Blue Ribbon Flies developed the X-Caddis over thirty years ago and it has become a staple pattern everywhere.

The X-Caddis is simple to tie. Only three materials are needed: the trailing shuck, body, and wing. By varying the hook size and body color an extensive assortment of caddis can be duplicated. To imitate an adult, the trailing shuck can be left off and the body wrapped with hackle or the fly can be hackled at just the head.

The Grannom (*Brachycentrus* spp.) is one of the first hatches of the spring that brings trout to feed on the surface. It's also called the Mother's Day Caddis due to its time of appearance. Grannoms often appear when Hendrickson mayflies are on the water, too. Watch closely to see which insect the fish are feeding on. You can replace the trailing shuck on the Grannom X-Caddis with a ball of bright green dubbing to match an egg-laying Grannom.

The Opal X-Caddis by Dennis Potter has a body of opal Mirage Tinsel that he feels can be used regardless of the natural's body color. Matching the size of the insect is most critical. Again, this pattern can be tied without the trailing shuck with a fully hackled body, creating an Opal Elk Hair Caddis.

Craig Amacker of the Madison Fly Fishing Co. in Wisconsin uses the Spring Creek Caddis on the streams of the Driftless region. A CDC puff is added as an underwing to aid floatation. Again, colors can be varied as needed to match naturals, with olive and tan shades being the most common for the Driftless.

GRANNOM X-CADDIS

(Craig Mathews)

- **Hook:** #16 TMC 100
- **Thread:** Black 8/0 UNI-Thread
- **Tail/shuck:** Amber or gold Antron yarn or Z-Lon
- **Body:** Gray dry-fly dubbing
- **Wing:** Fine deer body hair

Note: To imitate an egg-laying Grannom, replace the trailing shuck with a ball of bright green dubbing.

OPAL X-CADDIS (not pictured)

(Dennis Potter)

- **Hook:** #16-18 TMC 100
- **Thread:** White 50D GSP
- **Tail/shuck:** Golden Z-Lon
- **Body:** Opal Mirage Tinsel
- **Wing:** Yearling elk

Note: The GSP thread does a better job at flaring the elk hair wing to help create the head.

CRAIG'S SPRING CREEK CADDIS

(Craig Amacker)

- **Hook:** #16-18 TMC 100
- **Thread:** 8/0 UNI-Thread, olive dun for darker flies, tan for lighter-colored flies
- **Tail/shuck:** Tan crinkled Z-Lon
- **Body:** Olive gray or tan Superfine Dubbing
- **Underwing:** Natural dun CDC puff
- **Overwing:** Coastal deer hair

Caddis are found across the Upper Midwest in a wide range of colors and sizes. The adults are recognized by the tent-like wings that are folded down and across the back. They are easily imitated by a wing of fine, stiff hair tied back and parallel to the hook shank. Kevin Feenstra photo

Left to right: Mattress Thrasher, Mattress Thrasher Parachute Variant

Mattress Thrasher

Stoneflies are locally important stream insects across the Upper Midwest. They are in the order Plecoptera, meaning "folded wings." They are found in cold, faster-flowing water where the nymphs can be found in gravel and leaf litter, under rocks, and on submerged wood. Unlike either caddis or mayflies, they do not have an emerger stage. Instead, the nymphs crawl to rocks, roots, and shoreline vegetation to molt into the adult. After mating, females return to the river to deposit eggs and then die.

Where they are abundant, stoneflies can be an important food source for trout. They are found in a host of Great Lakes tributaries, where the nymphs are targeted by steelhead/migratory rainbows. Winter trout also feed on them regularly. These can vary from the miniscule Early Black Stone to the giant *Pteronarcys*, or Salmonfly.

Stonefly hatches across the Upper Midwest don't come close to those seen out West. The tiny black stones of winter can start to hatch as early as January in significant numbers and will attract some fish, but don't bring fish to the surface consistently. They can be targeted by trout on some waters and then ignored on others.

The larger stonefly species don't seem to be in the abundance needed to bring numbers of fish to the surface. The mayfly assumes that role across the

Although larger stoneflies are not found in significant numbers in many Upper Midwest waters, fishing a dry pattern like the Mattress Thrasher will produce fish. Smaller stoneflies are abundant, but trout attention to their emergence is often erratic and unpredictable. This is likely due to the cold water temperatures when this occurs. Kevin Feenstra photo

region. But, if larger stoneflies are seen consistently throughout the day, trout may key in on them. If adults are seen, it often pays to fish a nymph first, as they will be making their way toward shore. Female adults return to the river at dusk to lay eggs. The dry can be fished with movement to imitate the naturals.

For dry-fly anglers, stoneflies are available to trout when they get washed or blown off midstream rocks, are laying eggs, or are spent and dying on the water surface. Their availability is quite localized, as some waters just do not have the right conditions for them. Often generic patterns such as Stimulators are used to represent the various adults.

The Mattress Thrasher is often classed as a Golden Stone adult, but serves well as a general stonefly imitation and attractor, being tied in a full range of sizes. It is somewhat Stimulator-like in appearance, but a simpler tie. This is another pattern that has a place wherever stoneflies are found.

A number of variations are tied having minor differences from the initial design. Legs were included on the original pattern, but are now often left off. Krystal Flash and similar materials can be added beneath the wing, or the hackle can be tied parachute style. All will catch fish on any given day.

MATTRESS THRASHER
(Unknown)

- **Hook:** #8-16 2XL-3XL dry fly
- **Thread:** Black 6/0 UNI-Thread
- **Abdomen:** Black dubbing; palmer the body with dun hackle (optional)
- **Wing:** Deer hair
- **Legs:** Pumpkin Sili Legs (optional)
- **Thorax:** Yellow or orange dubbing
- **Hackle:** Grizzly

Top, left to right: Olive Body Skopper, Skopper Cricket, Yellow Body Skopper, bottom: Schroeder's Hopper with Hi-Viz post, two versions

Top Hoppers

Terrestrial insects can be an important food source for fish in the late summer and early fall. As hatches wind down, trout and other fish are still looking up and looking for an opportunistic meal. Grasshoppers and crickets provide a sizable meal, and when they are available, trout and also smallmouth bass will focus on them.

Hoppers are located where rivers and streams flow through open fields and grassy areas. They are usually found in significant numbers and as the day warms up, their activity increases. They jump strongly, and some can fly when disturbed. Males of some hopper species jump straight up to attract females. An errant jump or wind can push them into the water, where they land with an audible "plop" that attracts nearby fish. A hot, windy day is best for hopper fishing.

In his *Nick Adams Stories*, Ernest Hemingway's alter ego experiences hopper fishing in the story "Big Two-Hearted River," set in Michigan's Upper Peninsula. Although hoppers are used as live bait, the story gives a vivid description of this style of fishing with an original, Upper Midwest flavor.

Hoppers are found in an array of colors and sizes. Patterns with mixes of yellow, tan, orange, and green in several sizes should be carried. Generally,

This Skopper was tied with olive deer hair for an area with olive-colored hoppers. This colorful brown agreed it was a good match for the naturals. Making minor adjustments to fly patterns based on needs is part of the creative process.

fish are not overly selective when feeding on hoppers, but it helps to have several options to use.

Crickets are solitary insects, usually found along smaller streams. They are often found along woodland fringes, being most active around dawn and dusk. Most are black or dark brown in color and are also powerful jumpers. As with hoppers, they fall or get blown into the water, which often triggers fish to their presence.

Art Winnie created the Michigan Hopper back in 1921. It was later called Joe's Hopper, as it was popularized by legendary fly angler Joe Brooks. This was one of the earliest terrestrial patterns, and Winnie is credited with being the first tier to use turkey wing quills in a fly pattern.

Hopper patterns have gone through an extensive evolution over the decades. One of the most popular hopper/cricket designs for the Upper Midwest is called the Skopper. It's quite convenient that the pattern can be used for both by just changing the color, with crickets normally a bit smaller in size. This is a creation by Michigan angler/tier Tim Neal.

Neal looked at a number of hopper patterns and combined their best features into a single fly.

Schroeder's Parachute Hopper is another favorite pattern for the region. Though of western origin, it is well suited to the Upper Midwest. It sits low in the water, but is extremely buoyant and highly visible. Tied in black it is also a cricket imitation.

Fish hoppers and crickets along grassy banks and undercut areas. Cast so that the fly lands hard, just as the natural insect would. Both hoppers and crickets can float a long time and will struggle on the surface. Long drifts with a bit of movement added to the fly can bring explosive strikes. As wind often carries hoppers out into the water away from the bank, it also pays to cast along mid-river cover on a windy day.

In smallmouth rivers, a similar scenario often occurs. In late summer, they will target hoppers and crickets just as trout will. Here you may find smallies blowing up on hoppers, while others will sip a drifting cricket imitation as gently as a wary brown trout. Patterns can often be upsized for smallmouth without a negative effect.

SCHROEDER'S PARACHUTE HOPPER
(Ed Schroeder)

- **Hook:** #6-14 TMC 5212
- **Thread:** Tan or yellow 6/0 UNI-Thread
- **Post:** Calf body hair or suitable synthetic fiber
- **Body:** Antron dubbing to match naturals
- **Rib:** Brown UNI-Stretch floss
- **Wing:** Brown or mottled turkey quill section
- **Legs:** Ringneck pheasant tail fibers, knotted
- **Hackle:** Grizzly

Note: Again, by changing body, wing, and legs to black we have a great cricket imitation. Using a synthetic material like Hi-Viz allows different colors to be used for the wing post and increases visibility on the water.

Top to bottom, left to right: Simple Ant, Simple Flying Ant, Para Ant, Sunken Ant

Ant Variants

Ants can be an important food source for trout at times. They are most active during the warm temperatures of mid to late summer. Ants can vary in both size and color, with both flying and non-flying varieties, so an assortment of patterns should be carried. Mating swarms or migrations of flying ants can trigger significant feeding events when they occur along a river or stream. Otherwise, ants are similar to other terrestrial insects that are blown or fall into the water from branches or off the shore.

Ants are poor swimmers. Some will float in the film, while others sink under the water. They should always be fished in a dead-drift presentation. Trout will feed on them in both situations, so sunken or drowned ant patterns can be useful. When they are abundant, trout often feed selectively on ants. Ants are always worth trying when you see trout rising but are not able to identify a specific insect

that they are feeding on. This is especially true in midsummer.

A pattern I'm going to call the Simple Ant in black is probably the most used ant imitation. It is simple to tie and catches fish consistently. The key is to be sure to emphasize the two body segments when tying the fly. You can also tie it with Rusty Spinner color dubbing and in a combination of both colors. On smooth water, trim the hackle on top and bottom so it floats right in the film.

Ant patterns can be made in a wide range of variations. The fur dubbing on the Simple Ant can be replaced with a synthetic dubbing like Ice Dub to give a flashy, sparkling appearance to the body. At times, this seems to help trigger strikes. You can substitute rubber hackle, Sexi-Floss, or similar material for the hackle legs. This works best on larger sizes. Below size 14, the fur and hackle pattern is best.

Black and brown foam cylinders are available in small diameters and are marketed as ant bodies. These certainly simplify the tying process, and some have white ends for the head to make them easier to follow in the water. In my experience they are not as productive as dubbed-body patterns for trout, but are certainly suitable for targeting panfish.

The Simple Ant can be easily made into a Flying Ant by adding a wing material in front of the rear body section. This can be hackle tips, CDC, poly yarn, Hi-Viz, Z-Lon, or a similar material. If you encounter a swarm of flying ants, try to match the size and color of the naturals as close as you can.

The Para Ant sits right in the film so can be really difficult to see. The hackle post is brightly colored to aid visibility on the water. Use this fly on flat, smooth flows and stubborn fish that are refusing other patterns. The Sunken Ant has a thread body for the body segments that are coated with UV resin. A wet-fly hackle can be used for legs. You can also sink a dubbed-body ant by adding a small split shot, 6 to 12 inches in front of it.

All trout love ants during the summer. This brookie was rising along overhanging grass and eagerly rose to a well-presented Para Ant. The addition of the bright wing post makes it easier to track on the water.

SIMPLE ANT
(Unknown)

- **Hook:** #10-20 standard dry fly
- **Thread:** Black 8/0 UNI-Thread
- **Body:** Black or brown, or a combination of the two, dry-fly fur or synthetic dubbing
- **Legs:** Dry-fly hackle, to match body color

SIMPLE FLYING ANT
(Unknown)

- **Hook:** #12-18 standard dry fly
- **Thread:** Black 8/0 UNI-Thread
- **Body:** Black or brown, or a combination of the two, dry-fly fur or synthetic dubbing
- **Wing:** White or clear Hi-Viz, Z-Lon, or poly yarn
- **Legs:** Dry-fly hackle, to match body color

PARA ANT
(Unknown)

- **Hook:** #12-16 standard dry fly
- **Thread:** Black or tan 70D UTC
- **Body:** Black or reddish-brown dry-fly dubbing, tied in two distinct segments
- **Post/sighter:** Red, white, or chartreuse Hi-Viz or similar material, tied in at front segment
- **Hackle:** Black or brown, to match body color

SUNKEN ANT
(Unknown)

- **Hook:** #12-16 standard wet fly
- **Thread:** Black, brown, or red 8/0 UNI-Thread
- **Abdomen:** Tying thread coated and built up with UV resin (can be black, brown, or red)
- **Head:** Black tying thread coated and built up with UV resin
- **Legs:** Black hackle

Note: You can fish the Sunken Ant alone or under another pattern as a dry-dropper setup.

Left to right: Crowe/Deer Hair Beetle, Cheeto Beetle, Fathead Beetle 2.0

Beetlemania

To quote Mat Wagner of Driftless Angler in Viroqua, Wisconsin, "Beetles and ants are insanely important. We use them from early spring through fall." Here we'll look at some patterns that are effective across the Upper Midwest. In her *Pocket Guide to Midwest Hatches*, Ann Miller writes that there are about 160 beetle species across the region. Luckily, we don't need to try to imitate all. A generalist pattern usually gets the job done.

There are a few aquatic or semiaquatic beetles, but land-based ones seem to get the most attention from trout. Most are clumsy fliers and will make unplanned landings in the water or are blown in from shoreline vegetation on a windy day. Size and color of the naturals vary, but a dark fly in size 12 through 16 is suitable.

Beetles remain active through much of the fishing season, so are on a trout's menu longer than most terrestrials. They can be fished to rising trout when no insects appear to be present and also drifted through likely feeding areas. Beetles do not swim well, so a dead-drift is needed. Fish them along grassy banks and under overhanging brush and trees.

The all-deer-hair Crowe Beetle dates back to the 1940s and is credited to John Crowe of Johnstown, Pennsylvania. It is a great fish-catching fly with a noticeable "plop" when hitting the water that often

This Deer Hair Beetle is a bit ragged after taking a number of fish. The pattern has been around for many years and still holds its own against foam patterns for effectiveness, but foam designs have the edge in durability. Both are quick and simple to tie.

triggers a hit from trout. One of the earliest beetle patterns, it is still a productive pattern today. The original design lacks durability and is hard to see on the water. Adding bit of Flexament, or similar adhesive, when pulling the deer hair fibers over the top and tying in the sighter helps significantly.

The Cheeto Beetle and Fathead Beetle 2.0 are recent designs that are both well-recognized fish catchers. The Cheeto Beetle is a staple pattern in the Driftless region and can overlap imitation as an ant, beetle, or cricket. A bit of colored flash on the abdomen helps trigger strikes. It floats great and is highly visible, so is well suited to faster flows.

Dennis Potter's Fathead Beetle 2.0 comes from the waters of northern Michigan. It features the addition of wings. At times beetles will have their wings extended when they hit the water, and this adds another level of realism. Potter feels that the oblong shape of the body is also an important component of the fly, as it gives a natural appearance. He also believes the wide-gap hook holds fish better.

CROWE/DEER HAIR BEETLE
(John Crowe)

- **Hook:** #12-16 standard dry fly
- **Thread:** Black 6/0 UNI-Thread
- **Body:** Black deer body hair, tied with tips back, then pulled over top and trimmed. Leave a few longer hairs on each side for legs.
- **Sighter:** Tuft of bright-color McFly Foam

CHEETO BEETLE
(Unknown)

- **Hook:** #12-16 standard dry fly
- **Thread:** Black 8/0 UNI-Thread
- **Body:** Strip of black closed-cell foam, sized to hook, pulled over top and tied down to form an abdomen, thorax, and head
- **Underbody:** Blue, green, purple, or red Flashabou strip
- **Legs:** Black rubber hackle
- **Sighter:** White and orange Hi-Viz or similar material

FATHEAD BEETLE 2.0
(Dennis Potter)

- **Hook:** #12-16 TMC 2487
- **Thread:** Black 8/0 UNI-Thread
- **Underbody:** Black Spirit River Fine & Dry Dubbing
- **Body/head:** Black 1.5 mm Fly Foam
- **Wings:** Gray EP Silky Fibers
- **Legs:** Fine black round rubber hackle
- **Indicator:** Fluorescent orange egg yarn

Left to right: Gurgler made from frog cutter, Gurgler from foam strip, Gurgler from Gurgler cutter

Gurgler

This is a fly of significance for several reasons. First of all it catches fish, all kinds, and lots of them. Next, it has a special historical context to the region. Finally, it is at home on waters all across the Upper Midwest and fits into two categories as both a trout and a warmwater pattern.

Originally called the Gartside Gurgler, it was a crippled baitfish pattern for saltwater striped bass. Boston, Massachusetts, cab driver/fly tier/angler Jack Gartside created the fly in the 1980s to fish his area waters. Gartside was known to have kept a fly-tying vise strapped to the steering wheel of his cab to tie while waiting for his next fare.

The fly was occasionally mentioned, but not well known outside of Gartside's area. Ohio-based fly angler Charlie Chlysta was always up to checking out new patterns and found it to be effective on local largemouth and smallmouth bass. He made a few tweaks to the pattern but kept the original foam back and front, the primary feature of the fly.

Chlysta has pursued the big browns of the Au Sable system at night for decades and is always looking for productive patterns. He received the nickname "Picket Pin" years ago from Rusty Gates. This was Chlysta's favorite nighttime pattern for a long time and he caught an impressive number of big browns on it. At that time, Gates Lodge kept a yearly score of browns over 20 inches caught and released. Picket Pin always had more than his share of fish up on the board.

Here's a gaggle of Gurglers ready for night work and more. Though designed as a saltwater pattern, it has become a staple in fly shops across the Upper Midwest.

Chlysta also loves to take patterns from other places and adapt them to where he fishes. The Gurgler is a prime example. He substituted a marabou tail and added rubber legs. Basically, he made an already effective pattern even better, at least for his needs. This version of the Gurgler proved to be a super-productive night fly as well as a great small-mouth fly. Smallies are Chlysta's other favorite fish.

Night patterns are generally cast down and across and allowed to wake across the current. Chlysta started casting the fly upstream along cover and swimming it back on a tight-line retrieve. This kicked up his catch score even higher—another innovation that is now used for fishing browns at night everywhere.

In *Rivers of Sand*, Josh Greenburg states, "Pin's greatest contribution to night fishing was introducing the rest of us to the Gartside Gurgler. The Gurgler has changed not only the flies we fish at night, but also the way we fish them."

Often now just called a "Gurgler," numerous variations are currently tied. The recipe given is Chlysta's favorite and the one most commonly used in the area. One unique feature is that the amount of noise a Gurgler makes can be changed by adjusting the angle of the foam at the head of the fly. The higher it is, the louder "pop" it will make. The lower the angle, the less "pop" and more of a "blurb." This is best accomplished by wrapping dubbing in front of the foam until it is at the angle you want.

As with most of Gartside's designs, this is an impressionistic pattern that gives the illusion of life. By varying size, color, and materials, it can be an injured baitfish, shrimp, frog, mouse, or a creature of the night. River Road Creations (www.riverroadcreations.com) sells cutters to tie Gurglers in a full range of sizes, eliminating the need to cut foam strips.

GURGLER
(Jack Gartside; Charles Chlysta version shown)

- **Hook:** #1-4 Daiichi 2461 or Gamakatsu B10S
- **Thread:** 140D UTC, to match color scheme of fly
- **Tail:** Marabou, with a bit of flash and Sili Legs, to match color scheme of fly
- **Back:** 2–4 mm sheet foam cut into ⅜- to ½-inch strips depending on hook size, per color scheme
- **Body:** F.staz or Cactus Chenille, per color scheme (optional: palmer with hackle)
- **Legs:** Sili Legs, one or two sets per side, per color scheme

Note: A more recent version uses Craft Fur for the tail, as it gives added durability over marabou.

The Gurgler found fame in the Upper Midwest as a night trout fly. Smallmouth are also active night-feeders and will consistently take a black Gurgler after dark. An effective presentation is to cast the fly down and across and wake it back across the current on a tight line.

White-Bellied Mouse

White-Bellied Mouse

Now generically referred to as "mousin'," night fishing for brown trout outside of hatch periods has evolved into a distinct form of fly fishing all its own. Chasing nocturnal browns has been practiced on the waters of the Upper Midwest for probably close to a century. Night fishing for big browns is now being practiced wherever they are found: the western US, the Ozarks, and even farther away.

A whole new group of fly patterns are being utilized that bring a higher level of realism to this special form of angling. Tommy Lynch's White-Bellied Mouse is a prime example of this. Although this fly has been around for about a decade, we can consider it the current "state of the art" in night flies. Owner/operator of Fish Whisperer Guide Service, Lynch is a night-fishing specialist and this is his signature pattern for targeting big browns on the rivers of western Michigan and other areas.

In the time it has been out, the White-Bellied Mouse has proven its effectiveness beyond just nighttime browns. It has migrated to the White River in Arkansas and the western US, and has become a staple pattern for Alaska rainbows. It is also a great pattern for both largemouth and smallmouth bass, making it another prime example of a crossover pattern that works for multiple species.

In waters with a lot of activity including anglers, canoeists, kayakers, and tubers, the largest fish in a system will turn into nocturnal feeders during heavy traffic times. Tommy Lynch designed the White-Bellied Mouse to target these fish after dark when they are out and hunting. When feeding times are limited, big fish need a big meal to meet their needs. Tommy Lynch photo

As a trout fly, this fills a food niche when the hatches of the big bugs like the Hex and Brown Drake are over. In order to survive, the largest trout become opportunistic predators in search of a sizable meal. Hoppers can fill some of the void, but big browns are still hesitant to come out of hiding during the day. Night gives a sense of security, and they can emerge from daytime hiding places and station themselves in areas to ambush prey such as mice and frogs.

Mice are nocturnal animals who wander and feed at night. Along a riverbank they fall in with regularity and will swim as they drift downstream, creating a commotion that alerts nearby predators. The presentation of the fly is the same way. It is cast at an angle upstream and swum back along cover such as logjams and undercut banks. Mid-river sandbars are also prime locations.

A stout rod and heavy tippet are needed, an 8-weight with 20-pound being the norm. Daytime knowledge of the fishing area is critical. Learn the hiding spots so you can target them efficiently after dark. After a fish is hooked, it needs to be kept from reaching its daytime lair. No finesse is involved when trying to keep a 2-foot-plus brown from diving back into a logjam.

Daytime mousin' for Alaska rainbows and bass fishing are a bit less stressful. The White-Bellied Mouse has plenty of life and movement as you wake or swim it across the current. The hits are often the same explosion you get at night. Big fish need big protein—they love to crush a mouse and this fly is one of the best to make it happen.

WHITE-BELLIED MOUSE
(Tommy Lynch)

- **Rear hook:** #2 Gamakatsu Finesse Wide Gap
- **Tail:** 3 mm wide rubber band
- **Rear body:** White rabbit strip, palmer wrapped, with sand or variant-colored rabbit strip pulled over top
- **Rear legs:** Orange round rubber hackle
- **Connector:** 30-pound FireLine braid
- **Front hook:** #1/0 Daiichi 2441
- **Front body:** White rabbit strip, palmer wrapped, with sand or variant-colored rabbit strip pulled over top
- **Back:** Strip of ⅛-inch thick brown or black Evazote foam
- **Rear legs:** Orange round rubber hackle

Note: Schultz Outfitters has a great YouTube video with Tommy Lynch showing how to tie this pattern.

TROUT WETS AND NYMPHS

*T*he use of wet flies and nymph patterns across the Upper Midwest has changed over time. In the late 1800s, the grayling anglers of northern Michigan and brook trout adventurers traveling the Upper Peninsula of Michigan, Wisconsin, and Lake Superior tributaries certainly used wet flies. The multi-fly rigs with gut-snelled flies were what was available.

As we have seen, the demise of the Michigan grayling and subsequent introduction of harder-to-catch brown trout triggered a shift to the more natural dry-fly imitations from the Catskill area. This prompted more recognition of adult stream insects, primarily mayflies, and more-realistic imitations.

The immature, in-stream stages of insects slowly gained interest from anglers spurred on by works such as Ernie Schwiebert's monumental Nymphs, which had much of its foundation in the streams of the Upper Midwest. Selective Trout *by Swisher and Richards also presented subsurface concepts of nymph and pupa designs that further increased the interest.*

Gary Borger's Nymphing *was published in 1979 and was based on his PhD work on insects in streams in Wisconsin. This was one of the first works showing how to tie specific patterns and then how to rig and fish them. The nearby streams of the Driftless area were a great laboratory for much of this work, and that area still has a strong tradition of subsurface fishing.*

Where we see nymphing playing likely, its most significant role in the Upper Midwest is in the steelhead fishery of the Great Lakes. Subsurface

Nymphing *by Gary Borger was one of the earliest works to give detailed information on fishing nymphs effectively. Borger presented a series of patterns and outlined how to rig and fish them properly in different situations.*

insect imitations receive top billing as the most effective patterns for migratory rainbows. Some of these patterns are very specific to insects and will be addressed in the next section.

Euro-nymph techniques and patterns have their proponents across the region, but this method is not practiced regularly by most anglers. Rather than actively targeting fish pre-hatch with nymphs, many Upper Midwest fly fishers are content to pick a section of water and wait for rising fish.

Wet flies are used at times, mainly in pre-hatch situations, but popularity is localized. This is not due to lack of effectiveness. Instead, it again reflects the preference for fishing dries when insects are active.

All that being said, we are going to start off with a classic pattern, the Wet Skunk, by Earl Madsen. This creation has kept a spot in fly boxes across the area for decades and is still considered a top fish catcher across the region. It is a generalist fly, imitating nothing in particular. Having a great silhouette and movement in the water, it could easily be classed as a streamer, too.

Fishing streamers for trout does play a significant role across the region. The Upper Midwest played a major role in the development of streamer patterns and techniques as they are practiced today. This process is ongoing, as we will see.

Top: Wet Skunk, two versions; bottom: Cryo Skunk, two colors

Wet Skunk

Earl Madsen's Skunk flies, both dry and wet, have held a space in fly boxes across the Upper Midwest for decades because they continue to catch fish. When I surveyed a group of guides and shop owners for their choice of top patterns, the Wet Skunk was on most everyone's list. Even with today's synthetics and other high-tech materials, this very basic fly continues to hold its own.

The Wet Skunk is very similar to the Dry Skunk, but without the deer hair wing. As mentioned earlier, it was possibly the first fly to incorporate rubber legs. This was a significant innovation in fly design, born from the need to scavenge materials from an assortment of local sources, this time pulling rubber band pieces from an old car seat or maybe a damaged golf ball.

The western Girdle Bug and the Wet Skunk are very similar patterns. Both were designed and introduced in a similar time frame, but no one seems to be sure which was first. The Girdle Bug is primarily a stonefly imitation. The Wet Skunk is a lifelike pattern, but is not an accurate replication of any living creature. There are various theories of what the fly imitates. It could be a drowned cricket, a large stonefly nymph, or possibly a hellgrammite. Regardless, it is a great pattern to use in

Is it a wet fly or a streamer? The Wet Skunk can be dead-drifted, swung, and stripped so bridges the gap between both categories.

high water, or when there is need to cover water and find active fish.

This is a fly that can be dead-drifted, crawled slowly, swung, or stripped. There really is no wrong way to fish it. It could be classed as either a wet fly or streamer, bridging the gap between both categories of flies. It is probably most often fished down and across on a tight line while adding movement with the rod tip. The Northern Angler in Traverse City, Michigan, refers to the technique as "twitchin'" and uses variations of the Skunk called Cryo Skunks that they refer to as "twitch flies."

There are a multitude of ways to create Wet Skunk variations. Proponents say the original version—black chenille body, white calf tail, white legs—works best on a cloudy day. Chenille colors can be changed, as well as leg colors. Marabou can be used as a tail, instead of calf tail or squirrel tail. The Northern Angler's Cryo Skunk pattern adds a flashy tail of Shimmer Fringe material. The original Wet Skunk had one set of legs per side; the current version usually has two sets per side.

Although designed as a trout fly, the Wet Skunk will catch a wide range of species. River smallmouth, in particular, find it especially appealing. A variety of panfish will hit it as well, and don't be surprised if a largemouth grabs one, too. Just about any opportunistic feeder is fair game.

Rubber legs are now standard on a wide assortment of freshwater and saltwater patterns that are used both below the surface and on top. Their fish-attracting qualities are unquestioned. Earl Madsen's Skunk flies helped to introduce this to the fly-tying and fly-fishing world.

WET SKUNK
(Earl Madsen)

- **Hook:** #8 2XL-3XL wet or nymph
- **Thread:** Black 6/0 UNI-Thread
- **Tail:** White calf tail or gray squirrel tail
- **Body:** Black chenille
- **Legs:** White rubber hackle

CRYO SKUNK
(Northern Angler Fly Shop)

- **Hook:** #6 TMC 3761
- **Thread:** Black 6/0 UNI-Thread
- **Weight:** .025-inch lead-substitute wire
- **Tail:** Pearl Shimmer Fringe
- **Body:** Wapsi Woolly Bugger Chenille or Sparkle Chenille; color as desired
- **Legs:** Clear/pearl-silver flake Sili Legs, two sets per side

Note: A multitude of variations of this design can be created from various types and colors of chenille-like materials and different rubber leg options.

Top: original Pink Squirrel; bottom: two Pink Squirrel variations

Pink Squirrel

The Driftless area covers parts of southwest Wisconsin, northeast Iowa, southeast Minnesota, and a bit of Illinois. It is a trout Shangri-la of cold water surrounded by numerous warmwater rivers and lakes. The last glaciers missed leveling the area and it is bisected with small, deep valleys, all with coldwater streams running through them. There are over 600 natural springs and thousands of miles of cold spring creeks.

Brook trout were the original natives of the area. Brown trout now dominate and can grow to impressive proportions. The area is close to several large metropolitan areas, but fishing pressure is rarely a problem. The rivers and streams of the Driftless hold an extensive assortment of aquatic life. This is one area of the Upper Midwest where nymphs and nymphing often take center stage.

One of the most recognized subsurface patterns for the Driftless region is the Pink Squirrel. This creation by John Bethke is a must-have for the area and will also catch trout pretty much anywhere. It is also a good steelhead nymph in larger sizes. There are numerous variations of this fly, but the original pattern from Bethke is given. The individual tier can certainly alter it as needed or desired, and a couple of variations are pictured.

The streams of the Driftless area show a wide diversity of insect life. Scuds provide a significant year-round food base for trout. Scud patterns can be fished throughout the year and produce fish.

The Pink Squirrel was not designed to imitate anything specific. Bethke's goal was to create an impressionistic pattern that would catch trout consistently. He definitely succeeded. It certainly has a buggy look, with an attractor color at the head.

My guess is that it might best imitate an egg-laying scud or sow bug. Both of these crustaceans are found in profusion across the waters of the Driftless area. They can vary in color from one location to another, and the palette of the Pink Squirrel incorporates an assortment of hues. Fox squirrel body fur has an abundance of guard hairs that help make an extra-spiky dubbing to imitate the legs.

A variety of spiky dubbing blends can be used, each giving a slightly different look. It is important to spin the dubbing in a loop for the body so the fur can be picked out or brushed to give it the proper appearance. It can also be tied on a jig-style hook with a tungsten bead as an update to the original pattern.

The Pink Squirrel is dead-drifted, often in tandem with another nymph such as a Pheasant Tail, making it quite an effective combination. It can also be fished in a hopper-dropper setup. You can also use the Pink Squirrel on stillwaters where scuds and sow bugs are present. Crawl it slowly and let if fall periodically to imitate a natural.

PINK SQUIRREL
(John Bethke)

- **Hook:** #12-16 Mustad 3906
- **Bead:** Gold, sized to hook
- **Thread:** Black 8/0 UNI-Thread
- **Tail:** Two strands of pearl rainbow Krystal Flash
- **Body:** Fox squirrel body fur mixed with amber Lureflash Antron and olive Ice Dub in a dubbing loop and picked out
- **Rib:** Red wire
- **Thorax:** Medium fluorescent shrimp pink chenille (Hareline CHM140)

Note: Whitetail Fly Tieing Supplies sells a dubbing mixture that is true to the original pattern. You can also find the original formula in Driftless-area fly shops.

Top: regular American Pheasant Tail with bead-head variation; bottom: two Euro-style versions tied on a jig hook

Pheasant Tail Nymph

Trout anglers worldwide carry some variation or possibly several variations of this pattern. Wherever trout eat mayflies, the Pheasant Tail produces fish. It is simple to tie with easily procured, inexpensive materials. Along with the Adams dry fly and Woolly Bugger streamer, the Pheasant Tail Nymph shares billing as one of the best trout flies ever

This nondescript fly had its origins on the River Avon, just north of Salisbury in England. River keeper Frank Sawyer is credited with creating the pattern in the early 1950s. The color and silhouette is a very realistic representation of the Avon's mayfly

nymphs. It proved to be extremely effective on the snooty brown trout of the area, but has been largely forgotten in this original form.

Sawyer's pattern was unique, as it used copper wire both for weight and to secure the pheasant tail to the hook. As the color of the natural pheasant fibers closely matched that of the mayfly nymphs of the river, Sawyer also felt that that the "glow" of the copper wire in the water matched the translucency of the natural insect.

The modern "American" version of the Pheasant Tail is attributed to the late Al Troth, a Pennsylvania native turned Montana guide. The addition of

Frank Sawyer's original version of the Pheasant Tail Nymph used copper wire instead of tying thread. This provided additional weight and Sawyer felt the reflection of the wire matched the natural translucency of the insect. The pattern is still effective today.

the peacock herl takes the fly to another level of effectiveness. The natural iridescence of peacock provides an extra fish-attracting sparkle.

There is a variety of different Pheasant Tail designs. Adding a brass or tungsten bead at the head of the fly adds additional weight and flash to the fly. Different materials can be used for the thorax; using Ice Dub for this is an easy way to give a different look. The Pheasant Tail also adapts well to a Euro-nymph design. Here a CDC fiber collar is added. The use of CDC is common on this style of nymph, the fibers giving additional lifelike movement.

Dyed pheasant fibers can also be used to give a different look to the fly. Black in particular is a key color, especially in smaller sizes where it can also imitate the various early season stonefly nymphs. The Pheasant Tail can also be a productive steelhead nymph, especially on the Lake Erie tributaries. Tied on a heavier-wire hook, like a Daiichi 1530, a size 10 or 12 black or natural Pheasant Tail with a purple or chartreuse Ice Dub thorax has accounted for countless Lake Erie steelhead over the years.

SAWYER PHEASANT TAIL
(Frank Sawyer)

- **Hook:** #12-18 standard wet fly or nymph
- **Thread:** Copper wire, sized to hook
- **Tail:** Natural pheasant tail fibers
- **Body:** Natural pheasant tail fibers
- **Rib:** Copper wire
- **Thorax:** Copper wire
- **Wing case:** Natural pheasant tail fibers

AMERICAN PHEASANT TAIL
(Al Troth)

- **Hook:** #12-20 standard nymph
- **Bead:** Gold or copper, sized to hook (optional)
- **Thread:** 8/0 UNI-Thread, color to match body
- **Tail:** Pheasant tail fibers
- **Abdomen:** Pheasant tail fibers
- **Rib:** Copper wire
- **Thorax:** Peacock herl
- **Wing case:** Pheasant tail fibers
- **Legs:** Tips of wing case fibers

EURO-STYLE PHEASANT TAIL
(Unknown)

- **Hook:** #10-16 jig-style nymph
- **Bead:** Tungsten, sized to hook
- **Thread:** Black 8/0 UNI-Thread
- **Tail:** Pheasant tail fibers
- **Abdomen:** Pheasant tail fibers
- **Rib:** Copper wire
- **Thorax:** Peacock herl or peacock Ice Dub; add bright thread as a hot spot (optional)
- **Collar:** CDC feather, wrapped (optional)

Top to bottom: Bob's Swimming Iso, Bob's Swimming Iso Beadhead, Iso Soft Hackle

Bob's Swimming Iso

Isonychia nymphs are found in rocky areas with fast current. They are powerful swimmers, able to move freely through the water column. To emerge, the nymphs often crawl out on a rock or move to an area of slower-moving water. Where present, Iso nymphs are available to trout for a significant part of the season and the fish recognize them well.

These nymphs are easily recognized by the light-colored stripe that runs down over the wing case and into their body. This gives them the second part of their scientific name, *bicolor*. The body color

varies from a purplish brown to reddish brown. This color scheme is well replicated with peacock herl.

The Swimming Iso is credited to Bob Linsenman, a fixture on the Au Sable River around Mio, Michigan, for many years, While best known for his work with Kelly Galloup on *Modern Streamers for Trophy Trout*, Linsenman fished a variety of techniques and patterns suited to the area. The Swimming Iso pattern fit his style well.

Linsenman fished what is known as the "Big Water" of the Au Sable, with lots of rocky areas and deep, fast flows—perfect Iso water. There are plenty of trout and no shortage of big ones. Selectively fishing these areas with this pattern will get fish, and the fly can be used anywhere *Isonychia* mayflies are found.

The pattern can be fished dead-drift, but strikes often occur at the end of the drift when the fly is allowed to swing and rise with a series of twitches added. It can also be stripped similar to a streamer. This works best in the slower areas adjacent to fast flows. Strikes can be vicious, as the fish are used to chasing these fast-swimming nymphs.

The Swimming Iso is tied with weight added, usually a black brass bead, but tungsten is certainly usable for the fastest areas. The weight can also be wrapped on the hook shank if desired. Having the fly in a few different weights allows you to adjust for depth and current speed.

As we know, the natural iridescence of peacock herl attracts fish, and this pattern is a prime example of that. The white stripe on the back gives good contrast in the water and brings to mind another great pattern, the Prince Nymph. We usually think

The white stripe on the wing case is a prominent feature of Isonychia *nymphs. On several species it extends down into the thorax. These nymphs are active swimmers and inhabit rocky areas with deep, fast flows. Kevin Feenstra photo*

of the Prince as a stonefly nymph due to its biot tails, but the peacock body and white biots on the back also bring an Iso nymph to mind. The Prince Nymph could have held a place in this book, too.

The Swimming Iso is also a pattern that adapts well to trout Spey use. With a few simple material adjustments, it can be easily updated to a soft-hackle wet fly. The swimming behavior of the *Isonychia* natural makes the fly a great candidate for swung-fly use.

BOB'S SWIMMING ISO
(Bob Linsenman)

- **Hook:** #10 Daiichi 1760 or 1260, or TMC 200R
- **Bead:** Black ⅛ inch (optional)
- **Thread:** Black 6/0 UNI-Thread
- **Tail:** Medium dun hackle fibers
- **Body:** Peacock herl with a strand of dental floss pulled over top
- **Rib:** Black wire
- **Wing:** Gray poly yarn
- **Hackle:** Grizzly hen

Note: This can also be an effective pattern for Lake Erie steelhead. Though Iso nymphs are not abundant on Lake Erie tributaries, the dark body / white stripe contrast has an appeal to the area's migratory rainbows.

ISO SOFT HACKLE
(Unknown)

- **Hook:** #10 Daiichi 1260 or TMC 200R
- **Thread:** Black 70D UTC
- **Tail:** Pheasant tail fibers
- **Body:** Peacock herl with a stripe of white thread or floss over top
- **Rib:** Black or copper wire
- **Hackle:** Gray partridge or grizzly hen

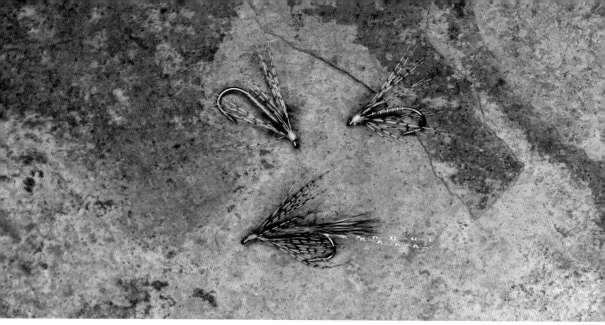

Top: Partridge & Yellow Soft Hackle, two sizes; bottom: Gray Drake Soft Hackle

Soft-Hackle Wets

This is the classic wet-fly design recognized by trout anglers around the world. Soft-hackle wet flies can be traced back to the late 1400s in the writings of Dame Juliana Berners. We do know that British and other European settlers brought this design along with them to North America and put it to use for the native brook and then grayling that they encountered. However, as dry flies became popular and then streamers entered the scene, wet flies fell out of favor.

Sylvester Nemes resurrected them from obscurity through his book *The Soft-Hackled Fly*, published in 1975. These flies are quite simplistic—often just a thin body and front hackle. They are impressionistic and do not imitate any specific insect, but are suggestive of both emerging mayfly and caddis. Nemes stated, "To be good, any sunken artificial must transform itself underwater into something alive." Soft-hackle patterns definitely do this.

Soft-hackle patterns are tied with feathers from various game birds including grouse, partridge, woodcock, and snipe. Other birds such as starling and more recently different hen chicken varieties have supplied hackle feathers. These usually come from the back, breast, or neck of the bird. The bodies were originally silk floss, but rayon floss can be used or various fur dubbings. The body is kept very sparse, often just tying thread reinforced with thin wire.

The hackle feathers are supple, but hold shape and do not collapse in the water. Only several turns of a feather are used that simulate legs or possible wings forming. Natural color patterns in the feathers add realism. With the hackle fibers tapering thinner toward the back of the fly, a natural tapered body is created. Hooks sizes are generally small, starting at a size 10 and going to a 16.

Famed Detroit, Michigan, rod builder Paul Young was a strong proponent of soft hackles. He

The Driftless area of the Upper Midwest provides endless trout-fishing opportunities. Most of the water is wadeable and has easy access. A wide range of fly patterns and different techniques can be used to catch trout. Craig Amacker photo

sold his "PHY Partridge Spiders" for 15 cents each at his shop. Dick Walle of Toledo, Ohio, tied and fished soft hackles on northern Michigan streams. With the recent introduction of trout Spey to the swung-fly crowd, soft-hackle patterns are enjoying a worthy renaissance across the Upper Midwest.

The Partridge & Yellow Soft Hackle is presented here for several reasons. The various mayflies generically referred to as Sulfurs are well distributed across the region and they match the normal hook sizes well. It is a reasonably accurate imitation of an emerging Sulphur when swung down and across. If fished upstream to rising fish, it can be a cripple.

Crane flies are found across the area and are abundant in the waters of the Driftless area. Yellow is the most common color. A Partridge & Yellow in size 10 can be used for this insect. They emerge starting in May and continue through the summer.

It may be that soft-hackle wets most closely resemble emerging caddis pupae. In this case, the size and color of the fly is adjusted to match naturals. Olive or orange floss are other popular bodies, along with pheasant tail fibers and various fine dubbing materials. A short thorax of peacock herl or dubbing can be added to help enhance the tapered silhouette of the fly. Hackle color seems not to be as critical as the body color.

Trico hatches are fairly localized across the region and overlooked by many anglers. Where they occur, swinging a tiny black-bodied wet with a white soft hackle will take fish. Although fishing these tiny mayflies is never easy, this is somewhat simpler than trying to maintain a dead-drift and track a miniscule fly on the water.

Kevin Feenstra's Gray Drake Soft Hackle incorporates a body of natural deer hair tied parallel to the hook shank in the true Michigan style. With the gray tying thread, this is a perfect match for a Gray Drake body. The Krystal Flash tail helps the fly stand out and attract attention in the large number of naturals present during this hatch.

PARTRIDGE & YELLOW SOFT HACKLE
(Unknown)

- **Hook:** #10-16 standard dry fly or nymph
- **Thread:** Yellow 8/0 UNI-Thread
- **Body:** Yellow silk floss, rayon floss, or tying thread
- **Rib:** Fine gold wire
- **Thorax:** Peacock herl (optional)
- **Hackle:** Gray partridge

Note: This particular pattern is specific to the Sulphur mayflies and yellow crane flies found across the region. Other key body colors are olive and orange in this design. Any various body materials and colors can be utilized, depending on the needs of the angler.

GRAY DRAKE SOFT HACKLE
(Kevin Feenstra)

- **Hook:** #12 Daiichi 1560
- **Thread:** Gray 70D UTC
- **Tail:** Two strands of pearl Krystal Flash
- **Body:** Sparse natural deer hair, tied parallel to hook shank
- **Hackle:** Partridge or grouse

Note: This design opens up an interesting range of opportunities, as it utilizes the classic Michigan parallel-tied deer hair body. As with dry flies, different thread colors can be used to imitate various mayflies.

Top: Coulee Scud, two colors; bottom: UV Tungsten Scud, two colors

Scuds

These small crustaceans are from the order Amphipoda and are found in the shallows of different types of waters. Scuds only inhabit clean water and can be a significant part of the trout's diet. They favor stable flows and temperature. In the Upper Midwest, they are most important in the spring creeks of the Driftless area, but are found locally across the region in other locations.

Scud colors vary widely depending on species, water chemistry, and aquatic vegetation. Olive, gray, tan, and pink are the most common. When they die scuds turn orange, much like saltwater shrimp. They are most active in low-light periods and at night, swimming in an erratic, jerky manner.

Scuds are usually dead-drifted during non-hatch periods. Fish them near weedy areas on an indicator rig. A quick kick through the weeds into a collection net will help you pick color and size of the imitation needed. Most will be in the size 12 to 16 range. You can drop a small imitation like a Pheasant Tail or Zebra Midge below the scud for an effective two-fly setup.

In larger sizes, such as 8 and 10, a scud pattern may also imitate a caddis or crane fly larva. Both

Brown trout are now the primary trout species in the Driftless region. The area's spring creeks support a diverse and abundant food base. Scuds are available year-round and are always on a trout's menu.

of these insects are also a significant food source in the Driftless area. There is also the thought that an orange scud is a suitable egg pattern, another big source of protein for feeding trout.

Key to creating scud patterns is replication of the shellback and legs. There are various commercial back materials and dubbing blends on the market and all of them are fairly coarse, allowing them to be picked out to imitate the numerous legs of the natural. The back can be as simple as a strip from a plastic sandwich bag or the latest high-tech UV resin. A wire or monofilament rib is sometimes used to create body segments.

Any survey of fly patterns will show us a multitude of effective scud imitations. There are two schools of thought on these designs. Some strive to be a very exacting imitation of the naturals, while others utilize materials to make the fly "stand out in the crowd." We will look at two homegrown designs from the Driftless region that employ these theories.

Mat Wagner of Driftless Angler gives us the Coulee Scud. It is done in six colors of Scud Dub

to cover the various natural hues anglers might encounter. A simple Scud Back strip ribbed with wire creates the body segments. Craig Amacker owns Madison Fly Fishing Co. and presents the UV Tungsten Scud. Amacker incorporates a UV dubbing and UV resin for body and back to make his imitations more noticeable. Both use a tungsten bead for weight, which can be in a bright color to add a trigger point and also imitate an egg pocket.

It's not a bad idea to carry imitations with both sets of characteristics. On any given day, trout may prefer one over the other. Often UV-based patterns perform better on a bright day, as their materials are enhanced by the UV rays from the sun.

COULEE SCUD
(Mat Wagner)

- **Hook:** #12-16 heavy-wire scud
- **Bead:** Gold, pink, or orange tungsten, sized to hook
- **Thread:** 8/0 UNI-Thread, color to match dubbing
- **Tail:** Partridge feather fibers
- **Body:** Scud Dub, color to match naturals
- **Rib:** Black mono or wire
- **Back:** Clear ⅛-inch Scud Back

Note: Driftless Angler offers the Coulee Scud in tan, gray, light olive, rainbow, light orange, and light pink colors. Scud Back to match body colors can also be used if desired.

UV TUNGSTEN SCUD
(Craig Amacker)

- **Hook:** #10-14 TMC 2488
- **Bead:** Fluorescent pink or orange tungsten, ⅛ inch for #10 hook, ⁵⁄₃₂ inch for #12-14
- **Thread:** Yellow 8/0 UNI-Thread
- **Body:** Tan, gray, olive, or shrimp pink UV Ice Dub, in a loop
- **Back:** Loon UV Clear Fly Finish, Flow

TROUT AND STEELHEAD CROSSOVER NYMPHS

*A*s mentioned earlier, where nymphs play a noticeably important role in the Upper Midwest is in the steelhead fishery of the Great Lakes tributaries. Calling these fish "steelhead" is disputed at times, as they do not spend time in salt water. What is undeniable is that these migratory rainbows have been present for over 150 years. There are numerous naturalized, reproducing populations as well as significant numbers of stocked fish.

Great Lakes steelhead will take both realistic and impressionistic nymph patterns. Blending a base silhouette and a trigger color can be effective. Be sure the hook is strong and sharp!

There is debate whether Great Lakes steelhead truly feed once they enter tributaries. Experience shows that they do if given the opportunity, other than when actually spawning. Some of the earliest accounts of catching these fish include fishing live "wigglers," which are actually Hexagenia nymphs. I've personally witnessed them busting schools of bait and even picking crayfish off the bottom while in tributary streams.

The Pacific salmon and brown trout also present in the Great Lakes are frequently encountered by fly anglers. Both will take nymphs as well as other flies. The big lake rainbows, though, have a particular affinity for a variety of dead-drifted, subsurface creations. Nymphing for steelhead began in the Upper Midwest. The patterns presented here represent the three major aquatic insect groups of the region: mayflies, caddis, and stoneflies.

Great Lakes tributaries range in size from tiny creeks to huge rivers like the Niagara and Nipigon. The insect life they support varies significantly from north to south. The imitations used can be very specific if there is an abundance of a certain insect. A good example of this would be the Hexagenia mayfly nymph and Rhyacophila caddis pupa patterns used in western Michigan rivers. We also find a significant number of stream-bred fish in these waters.

Where stocked rainbows predominate, a buggy silhouette in various sizes and colors can be an effective pattern. Here a pattern size and color may be selected based on water color rather than being a specific imitation. The feeding instinct is in the fish, but they are not imprinted to a particular insect. This is the situation on the southern Lake Erie tributaries where the majority of steelhead are hatchery bred.

The top requirement of a Great Lakes steelhead nymph is a sturdy, sharp hook. As the flies themselves may be small for the comparative size of the fish, 2X-strong hooks are the norm to minimize losing fish if the hook springs open during the fight. The goal is to get the fish in as quickly as possible so it can be released with minimal stress.

Given the unpredictable status of steelhead in the Pacific Northwest, the migratory rainbows of the Great Lakes will likely receive increasing attention from fly anglers. They are considered as one of the premier gamefish of the Upper Midwest. The various strains of these fish provide a nearly year-round opportunity to fish them in tributaries across the region.

Schmidt's Hex Nymph, two sizes

Schmidt's Hex Nymph

Ray Schmidt is legendary in the annals of Upper Midwest and Great Lakes fly fishing. He has been a river guide, fly shop owner, fly tackle sales rep and consultant, contract fly tier, conservationist, and much more. Over the decades, he has worn many hats in the fly-fishing realm, continuing to this day. He operated Schmidt Outfitters in Wellston, Michigan, a full-service fly shop, guide service, and lodging, just off the Big Manistee River.

A nephew of angler/tier Clarence Roberts, Schmidt was exposed to fly tying and fly design at an early age and is responsible for many patterns in use across the region. He was also one of the earliest guides to capitalize on the introduction of the Pacific salmon in the 1960s, which in turn led to the rediscovery of the oversize migratory rainbows we call steelhead.

There are stories of anglers catching rainbow trout in Great Lakes tributaries going back to the early twentieth century. Ernest Hemingway wrote about catching them in the St. Marys River in 1921. They fell into obscurity through the Depression and World War II, but with the successful return of salmon in the 1960s, the mysterious big rainbow trout appeared back on the radar screen. As their popularity grew, anglers simply referred to them as steelhead, just like their relatives from the Pacific Northwest.

Early fly designs were based on existing western patterns and produced inconsistent results. Bait anglers fishing live Hex nymphs called "wigglers" caught lots of rainbows. One of the earliest attempts at a legitimate Hex nymph imitation was tied by Ron Springs in the early 1970s. Called the Springs Wiggler, it didn't look much like a Hex nymph, but did have a buggy appearance and was more effective than earlier designs.

Schmidt was likely the first person to create a truly realistic Hex nymph imitation that caught

The Great Lakes tributaries of the Upper Midwest support good populations of steelhead / migratory rainbows that provide anglers a trophy fly-fishing opportunity. These fish have been in the Great Lakes for 150 years and many areas have self-sustaining populations. Aggressive stocking programs are also in place where natural reproduction is limited.

fish and could be produced commercially. After a period of trial and error to find the right hook to hold fish and find durable, lifelike materials, a design was settled on and the fly was introduced. He used the fly while guiding and later made it available for purchase.

Schmidt's Hex Nymph is fished dead-drift style. In the deep, fast flows of western Michigan rivers, this is often done with a tight-line nymphing technique similar to Euro nymphing called "chuck and duck." Schmidt helped to develop and then refine this method to its present form. These days Schmidt's Hex Nymph is often fished in tandem with an egg pattern and also under an indicator rig.

This pattern has also been responsible for countless Great Lake salmon over the years. Although they don't feed to survive once hitting a tributary to spawn, natural instincts will trigger some strikes on a drifting fly. Many a stream trout has taken the fly, too, as it is fished through a likely run.

SCHMIDT'S HEX NYMPH
(Ray Schmidt)

- **Hook:** #6-10 Daiichi 1710
- **Thread:** Tan 70D UTC
- **Tail:** Pheasant tail center barbule tips
- **Abdomen:** Sulphur yellow Spirit River Possum Plus dubbing, with gray ostrich and then pheasant tail fibers over top
- **Rib:** Copper wire
- **Thorax:** Spirit River Possum Plus dubbing
- **Hackle:** Brown hen
- **Wing case:** Pheasant tail fibers
- **Eyes:** Medium mono

Note: When tied on a size 10 hook, this is also a great Brown Drake nymph imitation.

Top: Possum Hex Wiggler; bottom: BTS

Possum Hex Wiggler and BTS

Kevin Feenstra is one of the most recognized guides and fly designers across the Upper Midwest. He is based on the Muskegon River near Newaygo, Michigan. The Muskegon is a year-round fishery that supports a wide assortment of coldwater and warmwater species. This gives Feenstra a long, extended season on the water, and he is an expert on the food base of the river through the seasons for all gamefish.

The Muskegon is one of Michigan's longest rivers, with a length of 216 miles. The section below Croton Dam is considered a tailwater, and this is where coldwater and migratory species are found. Above this, a full range of warmwater species are abundant. The mouth of the Muskegon forms a drowned river mouth, Muskegon Lake, which then empties into Lake Michigan.

Feenstra's fly patterns are creative, functional, and durable, and, most important, they catch fish. He is known for his ability to blend colors to be most effective under different water conditions. He was also one of the earlier proponents of Australian opossum body fur, which he utilizes in a variety of ways.

Feenstra is a strong advocate of pattern templates where the same base design can duplicate different food forms by simple material changes. These two patterns are a prime example of this. They are both

This bright silver rainbow just entered a Great Lakes tributary stream. Upper Midwest steelhead are available to river anglers nearly year-round, as a variety of different strains of fish are present.

considered steelhead flies, but represent two totally different organisms.

The Possum Hex Wiggler is not an exact Hex imitation, but gives the coloration and general appearance of a Hex nymph. It also incorporates movement with the articulated body. In this form it is also representative of an immature sculpin or various small baitfish. It can be dead-drifted, swung, or stripped and be productive.

The BTS, or Better Than Spawn, was named when Feenstra hooked several steelhead in a run just fished by a bait angler on the fly's first test run. It was designed to look like a chinook salmon fry. These are present in big numbers in the Muskegon and other Great Lakes tributaries where the eggs from the previous fall hatch in late winter and early spring. After absorbing their yolk sac, the fry gather into schools and slowly migrate downstream to the big water.

Fry are easy prey for steelhead, resident trout, and other gamefish who target them on their downstream journey. Most Great Lakes migratory rainbows are winter-run spring spawners, so this fry migration coincides well for hungry, drop-back steelhead recovering from the rigors of spawning. Again, the BTS can be fished multiple ways and will produce. Also, by changing the material colors, a variety of fry and small baitfish imitations can be created.

POSSUM HEX WIGGLER

(Kevin Feenstra)

- **Rear hook:** #10 4XL straight-eye streamer, cut at bend after abdomen is tied
- **Thread:** Tan 70D UTC
- **Front hook:** #6-8 Daiichi 1120
- **Tail:** Clump of Australian opossum fur
- **Abdomen:** Alternate sections of sulphur yellow Spirit River Possum Plus dubbing and clumps of Australian opossum fur
- **Connector:** 20-pound mono
- **Thorax:** Sulphur yellow Spirit River Possum Plus dubbing, with grouse, partridge, or hen feather pulled flat over top
- **Wing case:** Peacock herl
- **Eyes:** Small mono

BTS (BETTER THAN SPAWN)

(Kevin Feenstra)

- **Rear hook:** #10 4XL streamer, cut at bend after body is tied
- **Thread:** White 140D UTC
- **Front hook:** #6-8 Daiichi 1120
- **Rear body:** Natural grizzly marabou, tied as a tail and then wrapped around shank
- **Connector:** 20-pound mono
- **Front body:** Tuft of grizzly marabou, then UV pink Ice Dub
- **Back:** Silver Holographic Flashabou, tied in as a wing case on front hook; pull over body, then pull back, tie down, and trim a few fibers on each side as pectoral fins
- **Eyes:** Medium mono

Note: Changing the color and type of the dubbing on the front body segment allows different baitfish colorations to be created quickly and easily.

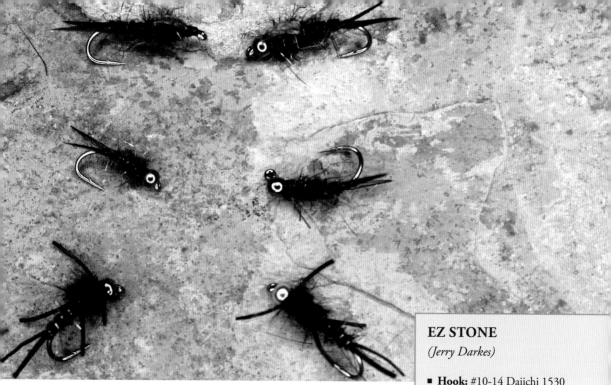

Top, left to right: Great Lakes Simple Stone, Great Lakes Simple Stone Beadhead; middle: Beadhead EZ Stone, Jigged EZ Stone; bottom: Beadhead Sexi Stone, two sizes

EZ STONE
(Jerry Darkes)

- **Hook:** #10-14 Daiichi 1530
- **Bead:** Black, sized to hook
- **Thread:** Black 70D UTC
- **Tail:** Black goose biots
- **Body:** Black Hare-Tron Dubbin or Stonefly Blend, in a loop
- **Rib:** Black wire
- **Collar:** Body dubbing, brushed out

Black Stones

Stoneflies are present in nearly all Great Lakes tributaries, varying in size from the miniscule Tiny Winter Black to the Giant *Pteronarcys*. Assorted other species fill the size gap. Stoneflies are normally found in moving water, with Rocky riffles and gravel areas as primary locations, where nymphs lie in gravel, in leaf litter, and under large rocks. If dislodged, they may drift in the current for a distance before settling in a new location. *Pteronarcys* nymphs often curl up into a ball when drifting.

Stonefly nymphs do not emerge in the water. Instead, they crawl out onto rocks, wood, or vegetation to hatch and develop into the adult form. During hatch periods the empty shucks are often seen. This is uncommon to see during steelhead time, as the only stoneflies hatching are the smallest species.

Stonefly nymph imitations can be quite complex, but these patterns can be simplified for steelhead use. The two V-shaped tails and tapered profile are the primary features required. The multiple wing cases shown on many imitations don't appear to be critical and add extra time to the tying process. As nymphs tumble in the current, a quick decision is needed by the fish to grab the fly or not. Tying "in the round" is a viable option, as we shall see.

Probably the most-used stonefly nymph pattern across the Great Lakes tributaries is Rick Kustich's

Simple Stone nymph. It is a essentially a Hare's Ear Nymph with a twin biot tail. Black is the primary color, but a Golden Stone pattern is also good. Also, remember that just-molted nymphs are very light in color, so a cream dubbing can be used, too.

Tying in the round gives a simple, effective imitation of the smaller stonefly species that are active during the winter and spring—prime steelhead time. Spin a spiky dubbing like Hare-Tron or a commercial stonefly blend in the desired color into a dubbing loop, wrap the body thin at the back tapering heavier to the front, then pick out or brush the front part for a collar. I call this the EZ Stone.

The Daiichi 1560 is a good all-around nymph hook. The Daiichi 1530, 1120, and 1710 are all 2X-strong hooks capable of handling large fish in small sizes. I prefer the 1530 for the smaller nymph imitations. Because it's 1X short, you can tie a small body, with a strong wide-gap hook. I have hooked and landed plenty of steelhead on the 1530 hook in size 14. The curved 1120 hook gives the impression of a curled nymph. The 1710 is the choice for larger sizes, especially if a bead is added.

Several species of small black stoneflies are abundant in Great Lakes tributaries of the Upper Midwest. Steelhead will aggressively target these nymphs. They are dead-drifted through suspected holding areas.

These flies are not normally heavily weighted; a bead adds a bit of weight and attractive flash. To vary the pattern, use a trigger color for the thorax. Ice Dub is popular for this. It can be a bright color or something subdued, such as blue or purple. The black abdomen and blue or purple thorax is a great combination in cold water.

A more recent stonefly nymph variant is the Sexi Stone. Here Sexi Floss is used for the tail and legs, simplifying the tying process even further. This has proven to be a very effective pattern that can be easily adjusted as needed

GREAT LAKES SIMPLE STONE
(Rick Kustich)

- **Hook:** #6-12 Daiichi 1560 or 1710
- **Bead:** Black, sized to hook (optional)
- **Thread:** 140D UTC for #6-8 hooks, 70D UTC for smaller hooks, color to match dubbing
- **Tail:** Goose biots, to match dubbing
- **Abdomen:** Hare-Tron Dubbin, Stonefly Blend, or similar spiky dubbing in desired color
- **Rib:** Brassie wire, black for black body, copper for other colors
- **Thorax:** Dubbing to match abdomen or Ice Dub in trigger color, picked out as legs
- **Wing case:** Mottled turkey tail or pheasant tail quill section

SEXI STONE
(Unknown)

- **Hook:** #10-14 Daiichi 1560 or 1120
- **Bead:** Color as desired, sized to hook (optional)
- **Thread:** Black 70D UTC
- **Tail:** Black Sexi Floss, tied in a V
- **Abdomen:** Black Hare-Tron Dubbin
- **Rib:** Brassie black wire
- **Legs:** Black Sexi Floss
- **Thorax:** Black Hare-Tron Dubbin or purple, black, or chartreuse UV Ice Dub, in a loop

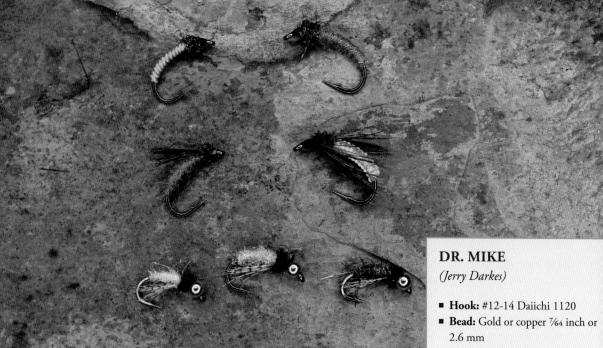

Top: *Antron Caddis, two variations; middle: PM Caddis, two variations; bottom: Dr. Mike, three colors*

DR. MIKE

(Jerry Darkes)

- **Hook:** #12-14 Daiichi 1120
- **Bead:** Gold or copper 7⁄64 inch or 2.6 mm
- **Thread:** 70D UTC, color to match body
- **Body:** Cream or olive Spirit River Brite Blend or caddis green Ice Dub
- **Throat:** Partridge, grouse, or mottled hen fibers
- **Head:** Peacock herl

Green Caddis

The caddis larva and pupa stages are the most important for the migratory rainbows of the Great Lakes. Caddis are abundant across the region and likely found in all tributaries. The most recognized of these come from the *Rhyacophila* genus and are generically called the Green Rock Worm or just Green Caddis.

There are a number of species that vary in size and in color from a bright green to olive. They are not net spinners or case builders, being called free-living. They inhabit fast currents with cold water and often drift freely in the current and become a prime source of food for both stream-dwelling and migratory trout.

Their abundance in some tributaries makes them a much-noticed food source for steelhead, and some will also be instinctively devoured by salmon. They are almost always fished dead-drift in tandem with another pattern like an egg or black stone. Depending on depth and flow, this might be done under an indicator or with a tight-line presentation.

Imitations can range from size 6 to 14 depending on the specific pattern. As with all steelhead nymphs, the hook is critical. It needs to be sharp and strong to hook, hold, and handle large fish in current. The Daiichi 1120 and TMC 2457 are both popular hooks, and anything equivalent to these is suitable.

One of the earliest and easiest imitations to tie is the Antron Caddis, also called the Green Caddis. This is a true "guide fly." The body is Antron yarn or dubbing with a peacock herl head. It doesn't get much simpler than that. The body can be yarn twisted and wrapped to look like segments, just finger dubbed, or dubbed in a loop, wrapped, and ribbed with wire. There are plenty of options and I can't say one is better than another.

If we add a soft hackle after the body and before the head, it becomes the PM Caddis, named after Michigan's Pere Marquette River. This would be more of a pupa imitation with the hackle added. An online search shows numerous variations of this pattern where the body is made up of various chartreuse-colored materials including vinyl rib, stretch tubing, or Diamond Braid, in addition to the yarn or dubbing. Again, they all work.

Being from northeast Ohio, I've spent thousands of hours on the Lake Erie tributaries referred to as "Steelhead Alley." Some of these streams are quite

This male steelhead is beginning to darken in color prior to spawning. Steelhead do not need to feed once they enter tributaries, but will take advantage of an abundant food source. A variety of insects are present in Upper Midwest tributary waters.

sterile, while others are surprisingly abundant in aquatic life. While doing stream insect samples, we consistently found several colors of small caddis larvae. I've never determined what the exact species are.

I tied up several different versions of these and settled on a pattern called Dr. Mike after my late, great friend Dr. Mike Bennett as the best. Mike was a psychologist, angler, and guide known as Dr. Steelhead. He fished the pattern extensively, and it is still very effective. Spirit River Brite Blend matched the colors of the naturals well, and an Ice Dub version was added as a Green Rock Worm variation.

All of these patterns are normally dead-drifted in tandem with some sort of egg pattern.

ANTRON CADDIS

(Unknown)

- **Hook:** #8-12 Daiichi 1120
- **Thread:** Black 70D UTC
- **Body:** Chartreuse to olive Antron yarn or dubbing
- **Rib:** Brassie gold or copper wire (optional)
- **Head:** Peacock herl or peacock Ice Dub

Note: If yarn is used, it can be twisted tight and will show a segmented body when wrapped up the hook shank.

PM CADDIS

(Unknown)

- **Hook:** #8-12 Daiichi 1120
- **Thread:** Black 70D UTC
- **Body:** Chartreuse Antron yarn or dubbing, vinyl rib, stretch tubing, Diamond Braid, or similar material
- **Hackle:** Brown hen, brown partridge, or grouse, wrapped
- **Head:** Peacock herl

Note: With the transparent nature of the vinyl rib, stretch tubing, or Diamond Braid, a chartreuse thread underwrap gives a brighter body color.

STREAMERS

*M*y personal definition of a streamer is "an artificial fly that is given movement by either the angler or the current moving it, and either imitates a living aquatic organism or features color, movement, and flash to attract fish to strike it." Streamer patterns are found in a wide variety of configurations and sizes depending on their application.

Theodore Gordon was experimenting with streamer designs in New York's Catskill-area streams as early as 1880; and while he is best known for his pioneering efforts with dry flies, we can also consider him the "father of the modern streamer." The basic pattern template he used, an elongated body and wing over top, is still the basis for most all streamer flies.

Streamer patterns can be fished to target the largest fish in a given area. This Driftless-area brown hit a sculpin-colored leech pattern. It is an effective fly across much of the Upper Midwest. Craig Amacker photo

The Upper Midwest / Great Lakes contributed perhaps the most influential streamer design ever created, the Muddler Minnow. The spun deer hair head was a new design feature that opened the door to an ongoing list of patterns that still continues today. We see a parallel with the dry-fly evolution that started in the Catskills and then moved to the Upper Midwest around the Great Lakes.

We also have to recognize two Pennsylvania angler/tiers for their contributions: Russell Blessing for the Woolly Bugger and Bob Clouser for his Deep Minnow. Along with the Muddler Minnow, this trio of patterns can keep an angler busy catching fish most anywhere worldwide in both fresh and salt water.

In 1999, Michigan angler/tier/guides Kelly Galloup and Bob Linsenman published Modern Streamers for Trophy Trout. *As Swisher and Richards's* Selective Trout *was for dry flies, this book quickly became the "bible" of modern streamer fishing. It outlined a complete system including flies, equipment, and presentation to target the largest trout in a river system.*

The concepts that Galloup and Linsenman presented are now employed worldwide for trout and have also migrated into the warmwater realm for a growing list of species. A new generation of fly anglers has emerged who have expanded the application of streamer techniques and fly pattern designs. New materials continue to appear and allow the creation of flies that we couldn't even imagine several decades ago.

Streamer fishing is a lot of work. It requires continuous casting with a heavier-than-normal outfit, often with a line where at least part or even the whole line sinks. The fly is then stripped back and then cast again. Those used to dead-drifting dries to rising fish are left with a sore casting arm after their first streamer foray. A bit of conditioning helps to minimize casting issues.

In addition to increased odds for a big fish, the visual aspect of fishing streamers in moving water has a big appeal. You are constantly on the move covering water, either wading or in a boat, targeting likely ambush spots with your cast. You track the fly when possible and look for the shadow of a following fish, or the fly simply vanishes with a take. You pull back and feel solid weight with that initial headshake and the fight is on. That's the fun of streamer fishing!

Streamers can now be employed in a wide range of waters from small streams to the open waters of the Great Lakes. With the ever-improving technology of modern fly lines and fly materials, few areas are off-limits. Flies can now be effectively fished to extreme depths and produce fish. Around the Great Lakes, for example, lake trout are consistently caught down to depths of 50 feet.

Top to bottom: Zoo Cougar, Rattlesnake, Stripped Down Muddler

STRIPPED DOWN MUDDLER

(Jerry Darkes)

- **Hook:** #2 octopus style
- **Thread:** 140D UTC, color to match body
- **Connector:** 30- to 50-pound braid
- **Front:** 20 mm Flymen Articulated Shank with braid secured to it
- **Wing:** Rabbit strip with hook attached Zonker-style, with Krystal Flash or your favorite flash over top
- **Collar:** Schlappen
- **Head:** Deer belly hair, loosely spun and rough trimmed

Note: My favorite color in this fly is pictured—barred white rabbit strip, pearl Krystal Flash, and a gray head—but any color scheme is doable.

Muddler Variants

The Muddler Minnow was the creation of Minnesota guide Dan Gapen. Designed in 1937 as a sculpin imitation, it was used to target the giant, migratory brook trout of Ontario's Nipigon River. The Muddler is to streamers what the Adams is to dry flies. Over the years, a wide range of variations have emerged, all with the defining characteristic of the original Muddler—a clipped deer hair head.

There are several ways that the deer hair head can be made. In some, the hair is tightly spun and packed, then carefully trimmed to shape. The Zoo Cougar follows this design, and the oversize head serves two functions. First, it gives the wide, flat profile of a sculpin head, a prominent feature of this favorite food of large trout. Second, it adds buoyancy to the fly, giving it a neutral density.

This was possibly the first fly specifically designed for use on a sinking or sink-tip line. Proper placement of the curved wing on the back is important to help it swim properly. The Zoo Cougar can be fished at various speeds with strips and pumps of the rod tip to create a variety of movements when retrieved.

Ray Schmidt's Rattlesnake adds a rabbit strip with beads for flash and weight and a trailer hook. All this makes it a consistent fish-catching pattern. It is a great choice when larger-profile flies are not getting looks. It sinks well and can be effectively used on a floating line. The beads may also help add a bit of noise. Colors can be natural or bright and flashy.

The bulk of the deer hair head also helps create a vortex effect that gives extra movement to the materials placed behind. Marabou, rabbit strips,

The Muddler Minnow was created nearly ninety years ago. It is considered the first streamer to incorporate a spun deer hair head. Numerous patterns with a Muddler-style head have followed.

Craft Fur, and other soft, flexible materials can be used. When the hair is spun loosely, it can still give a profile but will tend to soak up and hold water, thus sinking slowly.

That was part of the idea behind my Stripped Down Muddler, along with placing the hook farther back on the braid to eliminate a long hook shank. A short-shank hook holds fish better by minimizing leverage for the fish to work the hook free. This concept can be applied to most any streamer pattern.

This fly was first used to target coaster brook trout in Lake Superior's Nipigon Bay area. These fish are notorious for nipping the back of the fly. It has since caught a wide range of species and is especially effective when smallmouth are not willing to chase but will take a slow-moving fly. You can fish the Stripped Down Muddler just under the surface, mid-depth, or crawl it close to the bottom. I like it best on an intermediate line.

Even with the most recent materials used in streamers such as brushes, it's likely that spun and clipped deer hair will continue to be a part of the makeup of these patterns. It has been too important an ingredient in too many successful fly designs. Plus, it is easily obtained, cost effective, and relatively simple to work with after a bit of experience.

ZOO COUGAR
(Kelly Galloup)

- **Hook:** #2-4 TMC 300
- **Thread:** Black 100-denier GSP
- **Tail:** Yellow marabou
- **Body:** Pearl Sparkle Braid
- **Underwing:** White calf tail
- **Wing:** Mallard flank dyed wood duck yellow
- **Collar:** Olive-yellow deer body hair
- **Head:** Olive-yellow deer body hair

Note: This legendary pattern has been lost a bit in the multitude of current steamer designs, but it still produces as good as ever. The original color is given here, but it can be colored as desired. Be sure the flank feather placement is directly on top for the fly to swim and fish properly. The head is trimmed wide, rounded on top and flat on the bottom.

RATTLESNAKE
(Ray Schmidt)

- **Front hook:** #16 TMC 105
- **Rear hook:** #6 TMC 2457, snelled to 20-pound Maxima, with three to five brass or copper beads, and secured to front hook so rear hook is inverted
- **Wing:** Rabbit strip with Holographic Flashabou
- **Body:** Estaz, two wraps
- **Collar:** Deer body hair
- **Head:** Deer body hair

Note: Big flies are not always the answer—a small profile with lots of movement can be the solution. This is another classic pattern that continues to consistently produce. It is easily adapted to tie on a shank with wire to replace the Maxima connector. Tie this in light color, dark color, and bright color schemes to adapt to different conditions.

PEPPERONI YUM BUG
(Charles Chlysta)

- **Hook:** #4 Daiichi 2461
- **Thread:** Brown 70D UTC
- **Tail:** Brown or tan mottled or grizzly marabou
- **Weight:** Lead-free wire, same diameter as hook shank, on the front third
- **Abdomen:** Black medium chenille, tied heavy
- **Legs:** Black/white medium Centipede Legs
- **Thorax:** Burnt orange medium chenille
- **Hackle:** Cree or ginger saddle

Note: Bridging the gap between a streamer and a nymph, this fly also has characteristics of the western Yuk Bug and Rubber Legs nymph. This is Chlysta's favorite color combination. You can vary the colors as wanted for a natural look or as an attractor.

Top, left to right: Craw Bugger, two colors; middle: Pepperoni Yum Bug; bottom: Blue River Bugger, two colors

Bugger Variants

The Woolly Bugger goes way back on the time line to 1967. It was originally a hellgrammite (dobsonfly larva) imitation made to tempt smallmouth bass. The first ones were tied with a black marabou tail, olive chenille body, and wrapped in a black saddle hackle. It's doubtful Russell Blessing ever thought this simple fly would achieve the fame it has. This may be the overall, most recognized fly pattern worldwide.

The Woolly Bugger checks all the boxes: easily obtained materials, simple to tie, and catches fish. By varying color and size, it can look like any number of food sources for trout, smallmouth, and a host of other species. There are few fish, at least in freshwater, that can't be caught on this fly.

If there is a weakness to the Bugger, it lies with the saddle hackle. If tied in at the bend after the tail and before the body, the stem of the feather will often break and unwind after a few fish.

There are a few ways to remedy this issue. The first is to counter-wrap the body with a rib of fine wire or thin monofilament after the hackle is wrapped. You can also tie in the saddle hackle after the first wrap of the body. This keeps the stem protected where it is attached. Perhaps the strongest way to do this is to twist the chenille and saddle hackle together as a single piece and then wrap the body.

With any of these methods, tying in the hackle at the tip makes the fibers orient to the back and

The Woolly Bugger as created by Russell Blessing. This timeless pattern has been done in countless color schemes and variations. This original version is still one of the favorites.

get longer as you wrap to the eye. This gives a more natural, streamlined look to the fly.

Numerous variations of the fly have emerged over the decades. Bead-head, cone-head, and adding lots of flash are all seen regularly today. Rubber legs can be added. Body materials such as Sparkle Chenille, Cactus Chenille, and Estaz all give an updated appearance. Natural and dyed grizzly saddle hackle and schlappen help give an overall creepy, crawly, buggy look to the fly.

The marabou tail is also a bit fragile and subject to breaking off at times, especially when using hemostats or pliers to unhook a fish. Materials such as Craft Fur and arctic fox tail hair can be a replacement for the marabou. They are much stronger with a similar movement and can be barred with a permanent marker to create lifelike patterns.

We are going to look at three modern variations of this renowned fly. The Craw Bugger is one of my favorites. Use this wherever crayfish are found. Keep it on the small side, no more than 2 or 3 inches overall. Studies have shown that smallmouth prefer crayfish on the small side. The addition of the barbell eyes keeps the hook upright, minimizing snags. You can also add rubber legs to the side of the fly.

The Yum Bug is just a great fish-catching template. The original pepperoni color shown works great, but you can alter this as wanted. Color variations are endless, limited only by your imagination.

The Blue River Bugger comes from the Driftless region but will work anywhere. It includes some additional updates such as a dubbed body.

CRAW BUGGER
(Unknown)

- **Hook:** #4 Daiichi #1760, TMC 200R, or Gamakatsu B10S
- **Thread:** 70D UTC, color to match body
- **Eyes:** Barbell
- **Antenna:** Two strands of Krystal Flash, color to match the body
- **Tail:** Tan, olive, or brown marabou, Craft Fur, or arctic fox tail hair
- **Body:** Tan, olive, or brown medium chenille
- **Hackle:** Tan, olive, or brown grizzly saddle or Bugger Hackle
- **Legs:** Sili Legs, to match body

Note: This can be stripped, swung, or dead-drifted under a large indicator, or try the "crayfish hop" under an indicator.

BLUE RIVER BUGGER
(Craig Amacker)

- **Hook:** #6-8 TMC 5262
- **Thread:** Olive dun 6/0 UNI-Thread
- **Weight:** Copper round tungsten bead, 3⁄16-inch for #6, 5⁄32-inch for #8; eight wraps of .025 lead-free wire behind the bead
- **Tail:** Ginger or olive marabou, with three strands of copper Flashabou on each side. Wrap some marabou around the hook shank at the bend.
- **Body:** Peacock UV Ice Dub
- **Hackle:** Grizzly or barred ginger Bugger Hackle
- **Rib:** Medium copper wire, counter-wound

Note: Lots of color and movement here. You can cast this fly on a light, floating line, so it is well suited to spring creek use. Be sure to use a heavier tippet, as strikes can be quite hard.

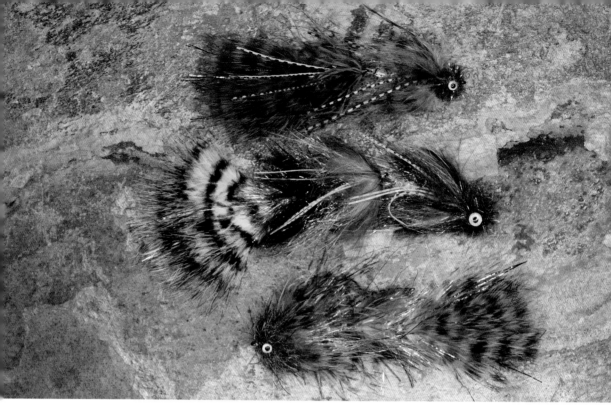

Top: Original Circus Peanut; middle and bottom: Chromatic Nut, two variations

Circus Peanut

A revolutionary pattern when first released, the Circus Peanut has achieved classic status in the streamer-fly world. This creation from Russ Maddin was possibly the first articulated streamer pattern and has influenced countless designs by anglers and tiers worldwide.

An avowed "streamer freak," Maddin is a well known fly designer and guide. The waters of northern Michigan have been a great proving ground for his work for many years. This pattern came from the need for a large fly with lots of movement that could be cast continuously and not tangle.

The joining of two shorter-shank hooks solved this issue, but created one problem. That was making sure the rear hook was secured so that it would not pull out from the front hook on a hooked fish. After being looped through the eye of the rear hook, the mono is doubled over and wrapped the length of the front hook, then coated with super-glue or Zap-A-Gap.

Maddin will tell you "The Nut," as he calls it, is basically two Woolly Buggers joined together with a few features added. It can be tied in any number of color combinations, but olive/black, olive/olive, and olive/brown are favorites from the dark spectrum. All-white and all-chartreuse are favorite bright colors.

An update to the Circus Peanut is the Chromatic Nut. This fly follows the original Circus Peanut template, but with a full range of newer parts and materials. This creates a whole new level of color,

The Circus Peanut is a great all-around streamer pattern. Not just a trout fly, it can be used to target different Upper Midwest gamefish. Smallmouth bass are another primary species.

movement, and flash. The fly now has multiple sections with holographic and UV materials being used.

These were designed primarily to target large trout, but will certainly work on other species. Overall size can be increased or decreased depending on the application, and colors can be altered and combined as desired. They are normally fished on some sort of a sinking line using a fast retrieve with plenty of rod-tip action added.

The Circus Peanut may be an older fly, but it is still a key pattern to target big trout. It is easily downsized for small-stream use and lighter rods. The Chromatic Nut might be the better choice on bigger water or under discolored conditions, and also when working up the apex predator ladder. If targeting toothy critters, use Intruder wire to connect the sections.

All of Maddin's patterns are extensively tested before he presents them to the public. Anyone looking to advance in the streamer game would be well advised to have these two patterns as part of their arsenal. An online search will show plenty of articles and videos featuring Maddin tying these two flies, and more of his fish-catching designs.

CIRCUS PEANUT
(Russ Maddin)

- **Front hook:** #2-4 TMC 9395
- **Rear hook:** #2-4 TMC 5262
- **Thread:** 6/0 UNI-Thread, color to match body
- **Tail:** Marabou plume tip, with Krystal Flash
- **Rear body:** Estaz, palmered with schlappen, with two barred Sili Legs each side at eye
- **Connector:** 30-pound Maxima
- **Front body:** Estaz, palmered with schlappen, with two barred Sili Legs each side at eye
- **Eyes:** Medium or large barbell, on underside of hook shank

Note: This recipe holds true to the original design. The rear hook is normally a size smaller than the front. Olive/black was the initial color combination, but tie up your favorite!

CHROMATIC NUT
(Russ Maddin)

- **Front hook:** #1 Ahrex Trout Predator
- **Rear hook:** #4 Ahrex Trout Predator
- **Thread:** 70D UTC, color to match body
- **Tail section:** 10 mm Fish Spine with tip of marabou plume, Holographic Flashabou, and UV Palmer Chenille
- **Second section:** 15 mm Fish Spine, UV Palmer Chenille, and wrapped rabbit strip
- **Rear section:** UV Polar Chenille, Senyo Chromatic Brush, and Sili Legs
- **Connector:** 30-pound Maxima with two 3D beads
- **Front body:** UV Polar Chenille, two sets Sili Legs per side, Chromatic Brush, and schlappen
- **Eyes:** Large Pseudo Eyes, on bottom of hook shank
- **Head:** Senyo Laser Dub

Note: This pattern utilizes an assortment of newer materials to enhance color, flash, and movement. Size and bulk are increased but little weight is added, so the fly is relatively easy to cast on a medium-weight outfit.

Left to right: Drunk and Disorderly (D&D), Mini D&D, Swingin' D, Mini Swingin' D. (See Appendix B on p. 132 for recipes for the Swingin' D and Mini Swingin' D flies.)

Drunk and Disorderly

This is a fly that is really well named. It acts just like a person under the influence—you're not quite sure what's going to happen next. Created by Michigan guide Tommy Lynch, it was designed to mimic the action and sound of a crank bait. When tied and fished correctly, it does just that.

It is a bit time-consuming to tie, but any fly designed to target oversize predators generally is. It is generally thought of as a pattern to target brown trout, and the D&D has caught *big* browns everywhere. The movement, flash, and sound trigger predatory instincts of a host of species including

steelhead, bass, pike, and muskie. I'm sure there are others, too.

The most unique feature of the fly is the deer hair head. Tied on a 60 degree hook, it is long, somewhat sparse, and trimmed flat. After being coated with UV resin, it functions as a crank bait lip, making the fly dive and swim on the retrieve. It's likely the fly triggers both a feeding and territorial instinct for a predator to want to kill it.

The combination of materials used—UV Polar Flash, rabbit, mallard flank, and Flashabou—unite to give color, flash, and movement. A glass rattle

The original D&D was designed to target the largest trout in a system. Typically, this will be a brown. The D&D has tempted giant browns wherever it is fished. Tommy Lynch photo

adds sound. Yes, this is a lure more than a fly, but we can say the same for most any streamer pattern. It's just that this takes things to a whole other level.

The fly is best fished on an 8-weight outfit minimum with a sinking line. Tippet should be at least 15 pounds and you can go heavier, as strikes are vicious. Along with a sharp strip, movement of the rod tip is added to maximize fly movement. I'd call fishing a D&D full-contact fly fishing and a true physical activity.

After the success of the original Drunk and Disorderly pattern, a down-scaled version was designed. The Mini D&D has all the features of the original, but in a size that is more comfortable to cast and work for most people. This smaller size is a great general-use trout and smallmouth pattern. It will also trigger aggressive strikes from steelhead once the water temperatures top 40 degrees.

Mike Schultz's Swingin' D follows the same concepts as Lynch's pattern—color, flash, movement, and sound—but uses a foam diver head instead of deer hair. Rather than made to dive, the Swingin' D has more of a gliding, side-to-side action.

It is often fished on an intermediate line to stay higher in the water column and is allowed to hover in between strips so its action is more like

a suspending jerk bait. Oversize smallmouth and pike were the original targets, but again, an assortment of predators will eat it. I have had good success with this pattern for Lake Superior's coaster brook trout and early-season lake trout in the Nipigon Bay region of Ontario. It can also be tied in two sizes, as with the D&D.

The tying process for both of these patterns is a bit complex and may be hard to interpret from the recipes. Schultz Outfitters has several YouTube videos that show the steps in detail and are well worth viewing. Give them a look and tie a few up!

DRUNK AND DISORDERLY

(Tommy Lynch)

- **Rear hook:** #1-2 Gamakatsu B10S
- **Thread:** Black or white 100D GSP
- **Tail:** Two webby schlappen feathers, with regular or Holographic Flashabou over top
- **Rear body:** UV Polar Chenille, with thin rabbit strip wrapped in front
- **Overwing:** Mallard flank
- **Connector:** 30- to 40-pound coated wire with two or three 8 mm 3D plastic beads
- **Front hook:** #3/0 Gamakatsu 61413 60-degree flat-eye jig
- **Front tail:** Regular or Holographic Flashabou
- **Front body:** Wrapped rabbit strip, medium glass rattle secured to top of hook shank (thread wrapped and glued), UV Polar Chenille wrapped over the rattle, Holographic Flashabou added over top of UV Polar Chenille, extending to end of front hook tail
- **Sides:** Mallard flank
- **Head:** Deer body hair, trimmed flat top and bottom, tapered on the sides, top coated with thin UV resin and cured
- **Eyes:** 3D, sized to head

Note: The recipe reflects the steps in tying. Colors can vary as desired, but light, dark, and bright combinations are a good way to start depending on your needs.

Top: Itty Meaty Thingy; middle and bottom: Squirrelsculpleech, two colors

Driftless Leeches

As mentioned earlier, the Driftless region is a land of numerous spring creeks located in an area of mainly warmwater rivers and lakes. Here you can find several aquatic organisms being especially important to the trout angler that are rarely mentioned elsewhere in the Upper Midwest. Among these are the already mentioned scud and now the leech.

For the entomologist, leeches belong to the phylum Annelida, which includes leeches and worms. The class is Hirudinea, specific to leeches. They are found in nearly all bodies of water. Some are carnivorous, feeding on snails and small invertebrates, while others are parasites, mainly on fish and turtles. They vary in both size and color, from 5 mm to over 450 mm in length with some mottled or striped in a full spectrum of colors. Most have a gray, olive, brown, or black base shade.

Gary Borger's book *Naturals*, published in 1980, includes a short discussion of leeches in the Upper Midwest and their importance as a trout food. He also mentions the use of strip fly patterns as imitations, a new concept back then, and attributes this to the late Royce Dam, from Franklin, Wisconsin. Dam was an award-winning fly tier and the author of *Practical Fly Tying*, published in 2002.

Borger's Strip Leech goes back to the 1970s. It's basically a fur strip tied Matuka-style on a standard

Brookies are the native trout of the Upper Midwest. They are still abundant in some areas, but have been displaced by browns in many places. This big Driftless brookie took a leech pattern. Craig Amacker photo

streamer hook. Still a popular pattern that can be easily adjusted for color and size as needed, it has also overlapped into the realm of an attractor fly. These days it is usually seen in larger sizes with a rabbit strip wing.

Mat Wagner of Driftless Angler says the Itty Meaty Thingy by local tier Ben Lubchansky is their top leech pattern. To paraphrase Wagner, "This pattern was designed specifically to be a leech that meets the needs of a short-line angler, but fishes great on the swing, too. The upturned eye and tungsten bead combine to give the fly an up-and-down motion when retrieved. This fly positively wiggles with life."

The original Itty Meaty was tied on a size 6 hook, and the Mini Meaty is done on a size 10. The mini version is well suited to the smaller trout waters of the Driftless. The original crosses over from larger trout streams to warmwater rivers, where it is a great smallmouth fly.

There are a number of leech patterns using pine squirrel strips as their primary material. Many of these are now being tied on 60-degree jig hooks and can be fished Euro-style with a tight line or stripped. Tied on the jig hook, snags are minimized.

The Squirrelsculpleech from Craig Amacker is a true micro streamer that can be a leech or baby sculpin depending on color. This can be fished multiple ways: swung down and across, stripped, short-line nymphing, or drifted under an indicator. In the Driftless these patterns are most often used early and late season, but are also a good option when the water is discolored after a rain. With a tungsten head they sink quickly for use in anything from pocketwater to larger deep pools.

ITTY MEATY THINGY AND MINI MEATY
(Ben Lubchansky)

- **Hook:** #6 (for Itty Meaty Thingy) or #10 (for Mini Meaty) Owner Octopus
- **Bead:** Black tungsten, 7/32 inch or 6 mm for #6 hook, 5/32 inch or 3.8 mm for #10 hook
- **Thread:** 8/0 UNI-Thread, color to match body
- **Body:** Black magic or gray olive Arizona Simi Seal
- **Wing:** Black or natural gray rabbit strip
- **Hackle:** Black or natural pheasant rump (#6) or hen or partridge hackle (#10)

SQUIRRELSCULPLEECH
(Craig Amacker)

- **Hook:** #10 TMC 3769
- **Bead:** Black, copper, or gold 1/8- or 5/32-inch round tungsten
- **Thread:** Olive dun or black 6/0 UNI-Thread
- **Tail:** Pine squirrel Zonker Strip, 1½ inches long, with lighter-colored marabou underwing and copper Krystal Flash
- **Body:** Same pine squirrel Zonker Strip used in tail wound around hook shank up to bead

Note: Good color combinations for the tail include black with chartreuse marabou and sculpin olive with ginger marabou. This pattern is easily adapted to a jig-style design with a hook like the TMC 413 and a slotted bead.

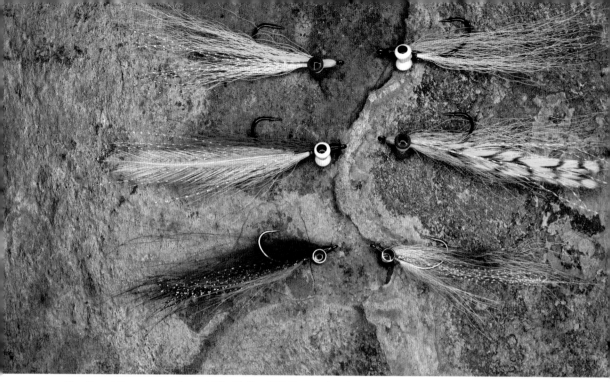

Top: Deep Minnow, two colors; middle: Half and Half, two colors; bottom: Foxie Deep Minnow, two colors

Deep Minnows

If we had to pick one single fly pattern to fish worldwide, in fresh and salt water, for all gamefish, Bob Clouser's Deep Minnow would likely be the choice. Few fly patterns have the universal acceptance by gamefish as this fly. Originally designed for smallmouth bass, the Clouser Deep Minnow is at home from the bonefish flats of the Caribbean to the open water of the Great Lakes and all points in between.

Across the Upper Midwest, the Deep Minnow catches a host of species. It is generally considered a warmwater pattern, but certainly can hold its own as a trout streamer. I'm a bit surprised it doesn't get more attention in this role, as it can be altered in a number of ways to resemble different baitfish and other aquatic critters.

Essentially, the Deep Minnow is a jig. The barbell weight provides the concentrated mass to sink the fly and, if painted, the eyes for a realistic baitfish imitation. Placing the weight on the top of the shank keeps the hook upright, minimizing snags and providing the up-and-down motion of the fly on the retrieve.

The Deep Minnow is usually tied on with a loop knot of some sort to enhance its movement. The barbell eyes should be perpendicular to the hook shank and sit flat. If the eyes twist at an angle, the correct movement of the fly is affected. Proper location of the barbell weight and securing it in place solidly are critical to the performance of the fly.

For freshwater use, most tiers have used the Gamakatsu B10S as the primary hook. The Ahrex

Though not normally a fly rod target, walleye will regularly take a Deep Minnow. They are often caught by anglers focusing on smallmouth in deeper areas of both lakes and rivers.

SA 210 Bob Clouser Signature Streamer hook is relatively new and made to Clouser's specifications for the Deep Minnow. Some of the newer jig hooks, such as the Ahrex PR 360, are also becoming popular. The jig hook does change the swimming motion of the fly, not necessarily better or worse—but different.

The original Deep Minnow pattern calls for bucktail as the back and belly of the fly. This should be around three times the shank for the back and two times the shank for the belly for proper movement and to minimize short strikes. Keep the bucktail sparse. Too much can kill the action of the fly. Many tiers way overdress this fly.

Secure the Krystal Flash in the middle, then pull it back to secure it on the hook shank. This keeps it from pulling out. It should be trimmed a bit longer than the belly hair. The back is then tied a bit longer than the Krystal Flash.

A popular Deep Minnow variation called the Half and Half adds a tail made of several saddle hackles to increase the length and profile for larger predators. Other materials such as Craft Fur or fox tail fur can be used for the back and belly. Different flash materials can also be substituted to give a different look to the fly. Lateral Scale is often used here.

The single most popular Deep Minnow color scheme is red barbell eyes, a chartreuse back, and a

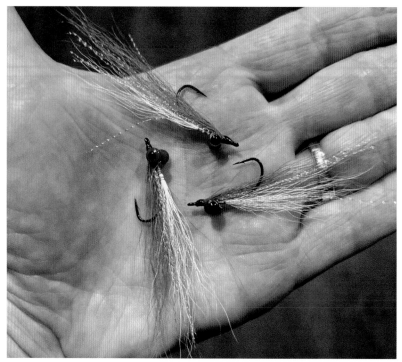

When young-of-the-year baitfish are abundant, gamefish may focus their feeding on them. Here it may be necessary to "match the hatch" and throw streamers similar in size and color to the naturals. The Deep Minnow can be easily adjusted to this purpose.

white belly with pearl Krystal Flash. This is a great imitation of the emerald shiner, a common baitfish across the Upper Midwest. White back / white belly, gray back / white belly, olive back / chartreuse belly, and olive back / orange belly are also used regularly. Color combinations are nearly endless for this must-have streamer.

DEEP MINNOW

(Bob Clouser)

- **Hook:** #1-8 Gamakatsu B10S or Ahrex SA 210
- **Thread:** 140D (#1-4) or 70D (#6-8) UTC, color to match back
- **Eyes:** Barbell with painted eyes, sized to hook
- **Belly:** Bucktail, two times the hook shank length
- **Back:** Krystal Flash, slightly longer than belly, with bucktail three times the shank length over top

Note: Keeping the bucktail lengths in proper proportion is important. Too short and the fly has little movement. Too long and there are short strikes or the material tangles on the hook.

HALF AND HALF

(Lefty Kreh)

- **Hook:** #1/0-2 Gamakatsu B10S
- **Thread:** 140D UTC, color to match back
- **Eyes:** Large (#1/0-1) or medium (#2) barbell with painted eyes
- **Tail:** Four saddle hackles, approximately three times the length of hook shank, tied in at hook bend
- **Belly:** Bucktail, two times the length of hook shank
- **Back:** Lateral Scale, slightly longer than the belly, with bucktail three times the length of hook shank over top

Note: This a great pattern for lake trout when they are up shallow. Pike and muskie will eat it, along with oversize smallmouth. It can be tied larger, but may become a bit difficult to throw. This size can be cast efficiently on an 8- or 9-weight outfit.

FOXIE DEEP MINNOW
(Unknown)

- **Hook:** #4-6 Gamakatsu B10S
- **Thread:** Burnt orange 70D UTC
- **Eyes:** Small red barbell
- **Belly:** Fox or coyote tail
- **Back:** Root beer Krystal Flash, with copper or gold Holographic Flashabou, and fox or coyote tail over top

Note: Fox and coyote tail fur is much finer and well suited to smaller baitfish imitations. It condenses a bit and has more movement. Different fur and flash colors and combinations can suggest a wide variety of baitfish.

Though designed originally for smallmouth bass, the Deep Minnow catches all kinds of baitfish-eating species. Lake trout can be targeted both early and late season across the region as they are feeding in colder, shallow water.

Bad Hair Day, two colors

Bad Hair Day

Sometimes simpler is better. Dave Pynczkowski's Bad Hair Day is a prime example. Just a few simple materials can make a super-effective, easy-to-fish fly. Here is another example of "imitates nothing specific, but looks like lots of things."

The Bad Hair Day catches a lot of different fish. Smallmouth, largemouth, pike, trout, steelhead, and coho salmon have all eaten it in freshwater. In the salt, tarpon, sea trout, jacks, redfish, and more will take it. It is a great fly to fish in the upper part of the water column.

An angler/guide based in Wisconsin, Pynczkowski designed the pattern originally for smallmouth bass, and it does that extremely well. It has also been one of the most productive patterns on my annual trip for the big coaster brook trout of the Nipigon Bay area of Lake Superior.

Two materials make up the fly: Extra Select Craft Fur and a bit of flash. The key in its construction is to reverse-tie the Craft Fur at the midsection and head. The fur is cut right down to the base, and most of the underfur is left in. When the fur is tied forward and pulled back and secured, the underfur holds the long fibers up. This keeps a profile to the fly, preventing the fur from collapsing around the hook shank. The fibers can then move and pulsate on the retrieve.

Smallmouth bass are the primary Bad Hair Day target, but it will attract trout and other species, too. A favorite presentation is on an intermediate line with an erratic retrieve where it is allowed to hover in between strips.

The Gamakatsu B10S is the hook normally used for the Bad Hair Day. The primary hook sizes are 1 to 4. Three clumps of fur are normally used. Flash can be put in with each section, but only a few strands are needed. Too much flash will reduce the movement of the fur.

White/chartreuse is a favored color combination for this fly: the two rear sections white, the front chartreuse. I have also had great success with all-white and white/chartreuse/olive. Obviously, color combinations are endless, and you can tie the Bad Hair Day in your favorites.

The length of the Craft Fur limits the size of the fly. To make a larger fly, the Bad Hair Day can be tied articulated by combining two hooks The rear section is a smaller hook, the front a size larger; e.g., 4 and 2 or 2 and 1. Join them on a length of Intruder wire with a 3D bead in between. Be sure to fully secure the rear hook to the front by coating the front hook shank with Zap-A-Gap or similar, then wrapping the wire the length of the shank. If you make the wire long enough so it can also be put through the hook eye, pulled back and wrapped, it will be absolutely secured.

One final hint for any Craft Fur pattern: After catching several fish, the Craft Fur will start to clump up. Combing it out with a toothbrush or similar item will separate the fibers and the fly will swim properly again.

BAD HAIR DAY
(Dave Pynczkowski)

- **Hook:** #1-4 Gamakatsu B10S
- **Thread:** 70D UTC, color to match front section of fly
- **Body:** Three sections of Extra Select Craft Fur, reverse-tied in the middle and front
- **Flash:** A few strands of Lateral Scale over the first two sections, sparse Angel Hair over the front section

Note: When tied correctly the fly has a distinct teardrop shape. The length and amount of Craft Fur used is proportioned to the hook size.

Top to bottom: Feather Game Changer, Leggy Boi, 5150. (See Appendix B on pp. 132–33 for recipes for the Leggi Boi and 5150 flies.)

Game Changers

When Virginia guide and fly designer Blane Chocklett introduced the Game Changer, it revolutionized the streamer game. Originally tied to focus on apex predators like muskie, the Changer has been size adjusted for a full range of species and applications in both fresh and salt water.

The heart of the Game Changer is the Fish Spine that allows the construction of multiple sections or articulations so the fly swims realistically in the water. The spines gradually increase in length from tail to head and are wrapped with materials that create water pressure. This makes each section move independently of the others, giving a natural swimming motion.

The application of different body materials has also allowed the creation of variations. Of particular importance has been the introduction of brushes. These are sections of various materials that are tightly spun into fine stainless wire. They incorporate an assortment of fibers, each with a different look, and simplify the tying process.

The fly is normally fished with a hand-over-hand retrieve so it is continuously moving and swimming. The larger sizes generally have two hooks, while smaller versions use a single hook. In recent years, several Ahrex models have become the "go-to" hooks for these patterns. These are light, strong, and super sharp.

Lake trout are not usually considered a fly-fishing target, but they can be targeted in a number of places across the Upper Midwest. A Game Changer fished on a sinking line is a great combination for lakers.

The Feather Game Changer is perhaps the most popular version. Here, hen saddle feathers are wrapped in front of a prop material. The width of the prop material and saddle feathers gradually increase moving forward on the fly to give a natural baitfish profile. Both natural and dyed hen saddle feathers are used depending on the desired color scheme.

Mike Schultz's Leggy Boi is used to target early-season pre-spawn smallmouth bass in colder water. This is when the largest fish of the year are often caught. It is designed to hover over the top of cover while the rubber legs wiggle enticingly. Pike will also crush this pattern.

Though not a true Game Changer, the 5150 from Tanner Ehlers utilizes the Fish Spine shanks to create movement in a vertical plane instead of horizontal as the other patterns do. This pattern was designed to specifically target bass—smallmouth in rivers and largemouth in lakes. It is fished on the bottom and can be hopped and crawled or allowed to sit and let the foam pull the fly up into a handstand, much like a crayfish in a defensive posture.

The original Fish Spine shanks have been updated to the Next Generation Articulated Shank that gives more movement, is easier to tie on, and is stronger than the original ones. The new triangular rear loop holds in a vise much better. The body sections can also be linked closer together. They can also be used as Waddington-style shanks for steelhead and salmon flies.

FEATHER GAME CHANGER (SINGLE HOOK)

(Blane Chocklett)

- **Hook:** #1/0-6 Ahrex S284 Minnow
- **Thread:** 140D or 70D UTC (finer-diameter thread on the smaller sizes), color to match body
- **Tail section:** Fish Spine Tail Shank with two small hen feathers or short section of marabou
- **Body sections:** Fish Spine Articulated Shanks, increasing in length to reach desired length
- **Body:** Medium or large (depending on fly size) Chocklett's Finesse Body Chenille with two hen saddles at front, width of chenille and hen saddles increasing toward front of fly
- **Head:** Secure body section to hook with Intruder wire wrapped the length of hook and coated with Zap-A-Gap, then add Finesse Chenille with hen saddle feathers

Optional: Single long hen feather on each side for pectoral fins or a jungle cock feather on each side for eyes

Note: There should be at least five total sections to the fly to get maximum swimming motion. These are usually tied as baitfish imitations, but attractor colors can also be effective.

Figure 8 (for size scale, the fly pictured is 8 inches long).

Figure 8

The pursuit of apex predators on the fly is an ongoing challenge for many anglers. In the Upper Midwest the muskellunge and northern pike are the primary targets. The interest in this fishing has increased significantly over the past several decades. There is now an extensive selection of fly patterns that we will call mega-streamers for this task.

One of the oldest and, in my opinion, still one of the best mega-streamers is called the Figure 8. This fly comes from the heart of Upper Midwest muskie country, Boulder Junction, Wisconsin. It is the creation of Bill Sherer, who runs We Tie It, a full-service guide service and fly shop. Sherer was one of the earliest guides to offer trips that focused on catching muskie with flies.

Though the fly was considered complex when originally created, it is quite simplistic compared to the pike and muskie patterns being tied today.

Several factors keep this a viable pattern in the current lineup of mega-streamers. First and foremost, it catches fish. It may lack the "bells and whistles" of some existing patterns, but as we know, there are times simpler is better.

Next, it is fishable for the average angler. The Figure 8 has great movement and attraction from materials that do not absorb too much water. When out of the water, the materials compress nicely to

Figure 8 🌿 **93**

minimize air resistance when casting. Being a single-hook design without rattles or other add-ons, it is also comparatively light in weight and castable on an 8-weight rod in its smaller sizes.

Many of the current mega-patterns have so much air resistance and weight to them, they need the equivalent of a 10-weight or heavier line just to carry them. Considering that these flies need to be cast continuously, many anglers are just not conditioned or skilled enough to do this for an extended time. The Figure 8 is a very forgiving pattern and a great choice for a starting mega-streamer. The angler can increase strength and skill with an excellent chance to catch fish.

The weedguard is a needed addition to the fly based on the cover where it is fished. It can be made from .030-inch nylon-coated wire (also available preformed from www.wetieit.com). To simplify this part of the process, I often use plastic worm hooks with a built-in weedguard. Both Gamakatsu and Owner have these.

Perch and fire tiger are favorite color schemes for the Figure 8. Black/red is a favored combination for muskie. Oddly enough, pink/red is a productive late-season color combination in tannic waters. For pike, red/white and chartreuse/white also get the job done.

Fly size is often a function of baitfish size. Early season, when the forage is smaller, you would opt for the 2/0 hook. For late season this could increase to the 5/0 hook. This will give a fly in the 10- to 12-inch range, possibly bigger. This size is still reasonably castable and able to attract a trophy-size fish.

Based on the numbers of fish it has caught, the Figure 8 is likely one of the most productive toothy predator flies so far created. It has certainly taken its share of bass, both largemouth and smallmouth, along the way. It may be one of the older apex predator patterns, but it is still going strong.

The biggest Great Lakes pike are best targeted right after ice-out when they move into the shallows to spawn. The Figure 8 is a great pattern at this time, as it is easy to cast and sinks slowly. It can be worked at a variety of speeds depending on the mood of the fish. Gord Ellis photo

FIGURE 8

(Bill Sherer)

- **Hook:** #5/0-2/0 Daiichi 2461 or Gamakatsu or Owner Worm Hook with weedguard in same sizes
- **Weedguard:** .030-inch-diameter nylon-coated stainless wire
- **Tail:** Long bucktail with Krystal Flash over top
- **Body:** UV Polar Chenille
- **Wing:** Icelandic sheep, then Krystal Flash and Holographic Flashabou over top
- **Belly:** Long bucktail
- **Back:** Bucktail with Krystal Flash over top
- **Eyes:** 3D

Note: Saltwater-grade bucktail is best for this pattern, as it is selected for longer hair than the regular type. The tier can also substitute various synthetic hairs if desired.

Yard Sale (for size scale, the fly pictured is 10 inches long)

Yard Sale

The Yard Sale takes us a way up the learning curve as an apex predator pattern that is articulated with a rattle incorporated. This style of fly is for the more experienced caster who is capable of tossing a heavy sinking-head line for an extended period of time. A double haul and water loading are both part of effectively casting these apex patterns. If you're not familiar with these terms, it's time to do some research and practice casting.

Matt Grajewski operates Adaptive Fly, a commercial tying business that specializes in fly patterns for apex predators. He lives almost in casting range of Lake St. Clair, one of the top muskie fisheries on the planet. His brother Eric is one of the top muskie guides on the lake. Between the two of them, they have many years of on-water experience chasing muskies and designing flies for them.

The Yard Sale is one of Grajewski's most recognized and productive patterns. It is mostly synthetic materials with a feather tail. This helps to reduce water retention and make the fly easier to cast for its size. It can also be tied as a single-hook design and scaled down in size for other uses like targeting bass and trout.

Weight and sound are added to the fly by attaching a rattle to the rear hook. Thoughts vary on adding sound to fly patterns. For predators, there is little doubt it can help attract them, especially in

The Upper Midwest is the native range of muskellunge. Matt Grajewski shows the Great Lakes spotted coloration on this Lake St. Clair fish taken on his Yard Sale pattern. Matt Grajewski photo

places with minimal water noise. While it may not be necessary, there really isn't a negative to adding sound other than perhaps a bit of added weight to the fly.

The design of the Yard Sale gives it a significant side-to-side movement when retrieved with long, strong strips. This swimming movement is the key to trigger strikes. It may take a bit of practice to get the maximum amount of movement from the fly. It is best suited for use in large, open-water areas where there is plenty of space to work the fly effectively.

Based on his extensive experience, Grajewski shares some sound advice for targeting muskie with flies. A general rule on fly size is spring = small, summer = big and small, fall = big. Also, don't overdress flies! More material means harder to cast and the angler expending energy. Work to get the right amount of materials without overdoing it. Targeting muskie with a fly is a marathon activity, so conserving energy is important.

Use a wire leader. Muskies are not leader shy—why risk a bite-off from the fish of a lifetime or leave a fly stuck in the mouth or throat of a fish? Grajewski's favorite is 7x7 braided wire.

Keep hooks sharp! Both muskie and pike have a bony mouth, so keeping hooks as sharp as possible is critical. Sharpen the hooks on new flies before fishing them, and touch them up regularly.

Finally, once you hook a muskie up, don't try to get it on the reel. This is where most are lost early in the fight. The rod is raised to crank line and drops slack, letting the hook fall out. Instead, play the fish by stripping and *always* keep tight to the fish. Feed line by hand if necessary, but unless it is an extra-large fish, they rarely run. Most action takes place boatside.

YARD SALE (DOUBLE HOOK)
(Matt Grajewski)

- **Hook:** 5/0 spinnerbait
- **Thread:** White or black 100D GSP
- **Rattle:** Large plastic worm
- **Tail:** Schlappen feathers and Flashabou
- **Rear body:** Flash 'n Slinky, top and bottom, tied in ¼-inch bunches and trimmed, with Flashabou on sides
- **Rear back:** Extra Select Craft Fur
- **Connector:** 65-pound Surflon with two large plastic beads
- **Front hook:** 6/0 spinnerbait
- **Front body:** Flash 'n Slinky, same as on rear body, with Flashabou on sides
- **Back:** Extra Select Craft Fur
- **Head:** Senyo Laser Dub, stacked top and bottom
- **Eyes:** ½-inch-diameter 3D

Note: This fly can be colored as desired. The color pictured is a favorite on Lake St. Clair. The fly is easily adjusted to a single hook and smaller sizes simply by reducing the amount of material to the hook size. On smaller sizes, wrapped lead wire can replace the rattle at the back of the hook to add weight and help the fly swim properly.

MAINLY WARMWATER

A look at several flies tied by the late Chris Helm. Working with deer hair is an art form all its own. Helm was a master at deer hair creations.

Warmwater fly patterns are those designed with a focus on species like smallmouth and largemouth bass, plus an assortment of panfish. The term "warmwater" generally refers to fish that are found in temperatures above 60 degrees F. Some of these species will also tolerate temperatures well into the 80s.

Both pike and muskie are often lumped into this category, but we could argue that they could be classed as "coolwater" species as they can handle water temperatures that are quite high, but also feed heavily when temperatures are in the 30s and 40s. This is particularly true with ice-out pike and late-season muskie.

We've seen there is a lot of overlap from the previous streamer section. Most streamer patterns can be used for an assortment of species, and the crossover from trout to bass, especially smallmouth, is very common. There are numerous patterns, though, that are targeted specifically to warmwater species and we will look at some of these next.

Surface patterns are definitely one of the top choices when targeting warmwater fish. The explosion of a bass on a popper and the gentle sip of a bluegill to a rubber spider are both part of this. These patterns can be very simple or may be some of the most intricate and time-consuming, as can be the case for certain deer hair designs. These can be a work of art as much as a fish-catching design.

Learning to stack, blend, spin, pack, and trim deer hair is a skill taken to another level with warmwater flies. Making a serviceable deer hair pattern is relatively simple. However, there are tiers who have turned this genre of flies into an art form all its own. The late Chris Helm of Toledo, Ohio, was one of the best deer hair artists ever and taught hundreds of students the skill to make artful, fish-catching patterns.

Deer hair patterns have been around a long time. Dr. James Henshall of Cincinnati, Ohio, is often credited with the creation of deer hair bugs for bass in the late 1800s. This is debatable, as there are references in the 1700s to natives of the American South using deer hair "bobs" for largemouth bass. Mary Orvis Maybury's Favorite Flies and Their Histories, published in 1892, features several color plates with deer hair body patterns.

An Upper Midwest angler and tier, Larry Dahlberg, brought the use of subsurface patterns to a new level. His diver designs influenced much of warmwater fly tying and fishing as we know it today. We can also look to Dave Whitlock as a driving force in this area. He took Dahlberg's designs and added his own influence.

Many of these patterns have minimal weight to them, though they do have surface area and often air-resistant materials in them. This makes casting them a challenge, so heavier line weights are used to carry them. A 7-weight is often the minimum line weight, with an 8- or 9-weight being a better choice.

Bass bugging is an American creation. Warmwater fly fishing is now as mainstream to the sport as trout. The list of targeted species continues to grow to the point where fish such as carp, freshwater drum, catfish, and others are considered viable targets. Fly creation and design is also following this path. There is a cadre of fly tiers and fishers who are taking the pursuit of warmwater species to a whole new level.

Top to bottom: Deer Hair Popper, two colors; Foam Popper, two variations; Zudbubbler, two colors

Poppers

Fishing poppers for bass is as American as eating hot dogs and apple pie. These flies, maybe more properly called fly-rod lures, are designed to float and make noise on the surface. The noise attracts fish, who then see the profile and movement of the popper, enticing them to strike it.

Cork bodies appeared in the late 1800s and the first commercial cork popper, called the Coaxer, came out of Chicago in 1910. Other cork-bodied bass flies came out of Arkansas and Missouri during a similar time period. These were a combination of cork and feathers attached to a hook—sometimes painted, sometimes not.

Cork was followed by more-sophisticated deer body and belly hair designs as tying knowledge increased. The deer hair phase accelerated into the 1980s and continues to this day. Tiers such as Pat Cohen, Steve Wascher, and others followed the lead of Chris Helm and Tim England and create deer hair poppers that are equally at home on a bass pond and on a fireplace mantle as a piece of folk art.

The key to a great deer hair popper is the density of the deer hair on the hook shank. In order to float well, it has to be tightly packed after being spun on the hook shank. This is done multiple times until the shank is covered. Then the hair needs to be

Poppers are often fished along transition zones where gamefish wait to ambush prey. Here there is a weed edge as well as a depth transition. This smallmouth could not resist a popper worked in the area between the weeds and drop-off. Dave Hurley photo

trimmed to the proper shape to "pop" effectively. This is another skill all its own.

The addition of rubber legs to poppers was a significant advance in fish attraction. It's hard to say who actually did this first. Earl Madsen is credited with the first fly with rubber legs, the Skunk in the 1940s. The western Girdle Bug dates back to the 1950s, so it would be after then. We do know that rubber legs are now a fixture on most all warmwater surface flies.

The use of closed-cell foam for popper bodies can be traced back to at least the mid-1990s. Upper Mississippi River guide Sheldon Bolstad designed the Blockhead Popper for smallmouth and whatever else would eat it. The Blockhead is quick and easy to tie with simple materials and catches fish—a true guide fly.

Michigan guide Matt Zudweg cut up flip-flops to make foam bodies. The tapered design has less surface area and is a bit easier to cast than the original Blockhead. With the addition of multiple rubber legs, the Zudbubbler popper is now state of the art in popper design. Zudweg also designed a tool, Zuddy's Leg Puller, to simplify the process of setting rubber legs in foam bodies. The use of the Leg Puller is pictured in the appendix.

A wide range of hard and soft foam popper bodies are available commercially. These are offered in an assortment of shapes, colors, and sizes to cover bass and panfish use. Various materials are combined with the popper bodies. Flashabou, Krystal Flash, and similar items give flash. Natural hair and feathers have synthetic counterparts that are often more durable. There are now even premade frog legs that can be added easily to give a realistic profile on the water.

The hooks used for many of the patterns are referred to as "stinger-style." This refers to a straight-eye, standard-length, wide-gap design. The wide gap increases the distance between the hook shank and point to reach around the larger jaw structure of bass and toothy predators. This allows a better hook set and keeping a fish secured during the fight. The TMC 8089 and Gamakatsu B10S are examples of this. Ahrex also offers this style of hook.

Various types of weedguards can be added to hooks for use in heavier cover. Hooks with a pre-attached weedguard can be used. A hard, stiff monofilament is generally used to add a weedguard. A quick YouTube search will show a number of ways to do this.

The flat front of the fly, no matter what the material used, makes the fish-attracting "pop" sound when sharply pulled on a tight line. The harder the pull, the louder the noise. Depending on the application, strength and frequency of the pulls vary. Generally, on stillwaters where the fish may come from a distance, the pulls are spaced farther apart to allow the fish time to locate the fly. On moving water, the pulls can be more frequent to trigger hits.

DEER HAIR POPPER
(Unknown)

- **Hook:** #1/0-6 Gamakatsu B10S
- **Thread:** 210D or 140D UTC for larger sizes, 100D GSP for smaller sizes, color to match body
- **Weedguard:** 20- to 25-pound hard monofilament (optional)
- **Tail:** Marabou or Craft Fur, with several strands of flash
- **Legs:** Large neck hackles tied just on front of the tail so that they curve to the outside, wrapped large neck hackle in front
- **Body:** Spun, tightly packed deer belly hair, with rubber legs added as desired in between sections of deer hair, trimmed tapering to the rear of the fly, left flat in front

Note: Solid colors including black, chartreuse, yellow, and white are all productive. Material colors can be mixed as desired. A frog coloration is the most popular.

FOAM POPPER
(Sheldon Bolstad)

- **Hook:** #1-10 Gamakatsu B10S
- **Thread:** 3/0-6/0 UNI-Thread, sized to hook, color to match body
- **Weedguard:** 20- to 25-pound hard monofilament (optional)
- **Tail:** Marabou or Craft Fur with large neck hackles tied in as legs on each side curving to the outside with a bit of flash added
- **Rubber legs:** Attach with X wraps in front of tail, at rear of body, or can be set in the body with a tool like Zuddy's Leg Puller (optional)
- **Body:** Hard or soft closed-cell foam, slid on to thread-wrapped hook shank, coated with superglue or similar adhesive

Note: Foam bodies may come predrilled for the hook shank. If the foam is solid, a hole can be created by heating a dubbing needle and pushing it through the body. A slit can also be cut in the bottom of the foam if needed. After the hook is inserted, glue is added and the foam pinched shut until the glue holds.

ZUDBUBBLER
(Matt Zudweg)

- **Hook:** #2 Gamakatsu B10S
- **Thread:** 140D UTC, color to match body
- **Weedguard:** 20- to 25-pound hard mono (optional)
- **Tail:** Marabou plume tip with a strand of Centipede Legs on each side doubled over and secured, marabou plume wrapped in front
- **Body:** Zudbubbler foam body secured to hook shank tight to tail in the back so hook eye is exposed in front
- **Legs:** Two or three sets of double Centipede Legs pulled through body

Note: The Zudbubbler is all about material movement. The rubber legs and marabou pulse and twitch with the slightest current or wind motion. Pops can be well spaced while the materials do their work. Color combinations are endless, but it pays to follow the "dark day, dark color / bright day, bright color" adage here.

Top to bottom: Feather Diver, two colors; Rabbit Strip Diver, two colors; Mega Diver (length as tied is 8 inches). (See Appendix B on p. 133 for the Rabbit Strip and Mega Diver recipes.)

Divers

Diver patterns are designed to do just that—dive under the water on the retrieve. By having a noticeable collar or taper to the fly's head, water pressure forces the fly under the surface when it is pulled. This can be done by stripping the fly or using the continuous hand-over-hand motion.

The deer-hair-head diver is credited to Larry Dahlberg, who developed this style of fly in the 1970s. Though his influence is understated and mostly overlooked these days, Dahlberg standardized the subsurface aspect of warmwater fly fishing with his diver designs opening the door. This is a true Upper Midwest creation that can also cross over into the trout arena.

Diver-style patterns also fit into salt water, where they are productive for an assortment of inshore species including tarpon, snook, and redfish. There are few patterns that have such universal application. Only a few simple modifications are needed to make a diver pattern cover such a wide assortment of use.

Dahlberg's first diver had a wing of just Flashabou in an effort to match the sparkle and flash of a Mepps spinner. This evolved into adding other materials behind the head including marabou and hackles as "kickers" like on a popper. Rabbit strips are used for a snakelike swimming motion. The Mega Diver, a creation for pike and muskie, features Big Fly Fiber, a material Dahlberg helped design.

Umpqua's Swimming Frog Diver is available at nearly all fly shops. It is one of the top-selling surface patterns for bass, both largemouth and smallmouth. A frog diver is a "must-have" for bass anglers.

A proper diver makes a unique "bloop" sound and leaves a bubble trail when stripped on a floating line. The kicker-style diver has rooster neck hackle legs that give the impression of a swimming critter, and the buoyant head lets it float back to the surface in between pulls. This makes for a perfect frog imitation, and this is the most popular color scheme in this version. A white Feather Diver simulates an injured baitfish.

The rabbit-strip variation can also be fished on an intermediate or sinking-head line as a streamer would be. This allows it to be fished at various levels in the water column. The buoyancy of the fly will let it hover in between strips. Much like a conventional angler's jerk bait, smallmouth in particular find this movement irresistible at times.

The Mega Diver can be made with a large profile due to the Big Fly Fiber. This material will stretch and contract when the fly is stripped, giving a great swimming movement. Added Flashabou gives sparkle and extra appeal. Neither material absorbs water, so even in an extended length it remains relatively easy to cast. It can also be fished from top to bottom in the water column depending on the line used.

There are also foam diver heads available that simplify the construction of diver-style patterns. These may lack the aesthetic appeal of deer hair, but function effectively. They come in solid shades, but

can be colored with permanent markers as desired. The stinger-style hook is normally used and is matched to the size of the foam head. For use in salt water, a stainless hook is substituted

A final tip, be sure these flies are tied on with a loop knot of some sort for maximum action. When targeting toothy critters, a wire bite tippet is a must. A weedguard on the hook is needed when fishing cover. This can be of mono, but should be wire when toothy predators are the target.

FEATHER DIVER, FROG COLOR
(Larry Dahlberg)

- **Hook:** #1-2 Gamakatsu B10S
- **Thread:** Olive 140D UTC
- **Weedguard:** 20- to 25-pound stiff mono (optional)
- **Tail:** White, cream, or yellow marabou plume tip, with several strands of pearl Krystal Flash
- **Legs:** One each olive, grizzly, and white rooster neck hackles per side, tied to curve to the outside
- **Collar:** Stacked deer belly hair, olive on top, white on bottom
- **Front legs:** One each olive, yellow, and white round rubber hackles
- **Head:** Deer belly hair, olive on top, white or yellow on bottom
- **Eyes:** 7 mm plastic doll eyes

Note: The deer hair collar and belly are trimmed flat on the bottom. The collar on top should be fairly wide and the head trimmed on top to taper from the front. Be careful not to cut off the front legs!

FEATHER DIVER, BAITFISH
(Larry Dahlberg)

- **Hook:** #2-4 Gamakatsu B10
- **Thread:** White 140D UTC
- **Weedguard:** 20- to 25-pound stiff mono (optional)
- **Tail:** White marabou plume tip
- **Legs:** Two or three rooster neck hackles per side
- **Collar:** Red Palmer Chenille
- **Head:** White or gray deer belly hair

Note: The Palmer Chenille is added to simulate gills and give some added sparkle to the fly.

Top to bottom: Foam Spider, two colors; Mini Foam Spider; Ol' Mr. Wiggly, two colors

Foam Favorites

The introduction of closed-cell foam materials created a whole new category for the fly-tying world. The use of floating foam in flies has spread across coldwater, warmwater, and saltwater use. There are dozens of foam patterns now that cover an extensive assortment of applications.

The use of foam in fly patterns dates back to the 1980s. *Tying Foam Flies* by Skip Morris was published in 1994 and was one of the original works on working with foam. This book presented a dozen foam patterns in detail, with information on a number more.

The first foam patterns were made with strips of foam secured to the hook shank. Rubber legs were added, with the Chernobyl Ant being one of the earliest flies of this type. A multitude of patterns

have been created off of this basic design template. Like many of the originals with fly patterns, the Chernobyl Ant has lost some of its appeal with anglers, but the fish still love it.

When preformed foam bodies appeared, this allowed simple and super-effective panfish flies to be tied with minimal time and effort. Only two colors are really needed: black and white. The white can be colored with a permanent marker in any way desired. Round rubber hackle, silicone-based Sili Legs, and Sexi Floss are all available in different sizes and colors and add lifelike movement to the fly.

The Foam Spider is a basic template for a great panfish fly. The body is secured to the hook by a combination of thread and superglue or Zap-A-Gap. Adding body segments is done by wrapping are targeting panfish, trout, or bass, there is a foam pattern for the task. It will be interesting to see what the next generation of foam flies looks like.

FOAM SPIDER

(Unknown)

- **Hook:** #10-16 standard dry fly
- **Thread:** 70D UTC, color to match body
- **Body:** Black or white foam spider body, colored with markers as desired
- **Legs:** Rubber hackle, Sili Legs, or Sexi Floss

Note: Fine rubber hackle, fine Sexi Floss, or rubber Nymph Legs work best on the small hook sizes. To form the body, wrap a thread base and coat with superglue, push the bottom of the body on the top of the hook shank, and secure with thread wraps in the middle of the body.

OL' MR. WIGGLY

(Charlie Piette)

- **Hook:** #2-6 Daiichi 2461 or Gamakatsu B10S
- **Thread:** 70D UTC, color to match body
- **Tail:** Orange Sili Legs, one strand each side (optional)
- **Underbody:** Ice Dub
- **Body:** 2 mm foam strip, cut to approximately half the hook gap width and 4 inches long, folded and tied in three segments
- **Legs:** Fine rubber hackle or Nymph Legs, two or three strands per side, tied in at middle and trimmed
- **Wings:** Sili Legs, three strands per side, tied in the middle
- **Indicator:** 2 mm yellow foam strip (optional)

Note: The body is usually tied in three sections with the folded part of the foam as the head. Dub and wrap the underbody a section at a time, as this eliminates any visible thread in between sections. Trim the body to a point extending a bit past the bend of the hook.

Palm-size bluegill and Foam Spiders are a favorite Upper Midwest fly-fishing combination. Countless opportunities across the region are available, and this is great way to start off beginning anglers.

thread. Different types of rubber legs give different looks. Smaller "mini spiders" will often attract trout along with panfish. Many a hefty bass has also decided a Foam Spider was a tasty tidbit and gently sucked in the tiny bug, surprising a bluegill angler.

Other sheet materials like Loco Foam are available that have a metallic or pearlescent coating on them. These can add a whole new dimension to fly appearance. This is reflected in the updated versions of Ol' Mr. Wiggly, a true Upper Midwest original pattern. This pattern comes from Charlie Piette, who was shop manager and a guide with Tight Lines Fly Fishing of DePere, Wisconsin.

The use of the metallic type of foam gives the pattern the unmistakable appearance of a dragonfly or damselfly. These can be a prime target for bass and panfish when they are present. It is also indicative of a move to more-subtle surface patterns for bass where they are getting overexposed to loud poppers.

Foam flies have earned numerous spots in the boxes of Upper Midwest fly fishers. Whether you

Top: Clawdad, two colors (on ends), Exo Skin Clawdad (middle); bottom: Swing Craw, two colors. (See Appendix B on p. 133 for Exo Skin and Swing Craw recipes.)

Crayfish

In the review of previous patterns, we have already seen the Craw Bugger. Picking a "best" crayfish pattern was not an easy task, for several reasons. First, there are a lot of patterns to choose from. My *Essential Flies for the Great Lakes Region* had twenty crayfish patterns in it, all of which are fish catchers. Some are better suited for stripping, others for dead-drifting. Some are realistic, while others are more generalist, resembling crayfish.

Be cautious with crayfish flies. Some that look the best in hand may not perform well while actually fishing them. If there are stiff materials involved, they tend to spin in the water if stripped too rapidly or when the current is too fast. This makes them pretty much useless. The fly needs to be lifelike at all times

A crayfish fly might be swung, stripped, hopped, or dead-drifted on any given day. Rather than a specific fly for each style of use, having one that performs all of these well makes sense. If we can cover these presentations and then only adjust color and size, we simplify the process.

At the risk of angering some of the great smallmouth guides across the Upper Midwest, in the end the pattern I chose may not be familiar to a lot of you, but it is a good one. Actually, it's a really good

The Clawdad was designed for smallmouth bass, but will take any fish that eats crayfish. Look for crayfish patterns that are relatively small (less than 3 inches in length) to be most effective. Also, try to match the color of the crayfish in the waters you are fishing. Eric Corya photo

crayfish fly and worth being called "the best." The Clawdad comes to us from the late Chuck Kraft, a longtime guide / fly designer from Virginia.

The Clawdad is semi-realistic, relatively easy to tie, and covers all different presentation needs. It can be easily adjusted for size and color, and the hook rides upright so it can be worked on the bottom. It can be stripped hard and fast or slowly crawled. The rubber legs add the illusion of life with any little twitch or pulse of the current. In addition to smallmouth, it can take largemouth, carp, trout, and even lake-run rainbows.

If there is a downside to this pattern, it is finding the claws or pincers to tie the fly. Referred to as Clawdad Claws or Tails, most fly shops do not stock these, but they are easily obtainable online from Eastern Trophies Fly Fishing, Mossy Creek Fly Fishing, Pat Cohen, and several other suppliers. These claws allow matching Kraft's original design.

With a bit of imagination, this basic design template allows for the creation of several productive variations from the original pattern. One of these is presented by Eric Corya, aka Carpstalker on Instagram. Corya fashions the pincers from Kiley's Exo Skin and the body from Squishenille to give an updated look to this pattern. A variation can also be made by using a short section of rabbit strip for pincers, with the body tied per Kraft's original pattern incorporating the rubber legs.

The Swing Craw is an offshoot of the Bad Hair Day. It also earns a spot for its ease of construction, effectiveness, and versatility. Strip it, dead-drift it, or swing it. With simple materials and a fish-catching design, it is a winner.

CLAWDAD
(Chuck Kraft)

- **Hook:** #2-6 streamer hook
- **Thread:** 140D UTC, color to match body
- **Eyes:** Medium or small plain barbell
- **Head:** Chenille, wrapped from halfway around hook bend to just across from hook point
- **Claws:** Clawdad Claws, sized to hook
- **Body:** Medium chenille, wrapped to form body and around eyes
- **Legs:** Round rubber legs

Note: The Clawdad Claws come in three sizes and seven colors, so there are plenty of color and size combination options. To attach the claws, run the hook point through the hole in the claws and seat on top of the chenille, then secure in front of the head. The original pattern had solid-color rubber legs, but barred legs and also Sili Legs can be used to create a variety of color combinations.

Top, left to right: Pollywog, Standing Hampton; bottom: Mojo Mulberry

Carp Candy

For better or worse, carp are an established part of the angling landscape across the Upper Midwest. Two types are of interest to fly anglers: the common carp and grass carp. The common carp arrived in the United States from Europe in 1877 as a replacement for native species that had been depleted by overfishing and habitat loss. They are well distributed across the region, from small streams to the waters of the Great Lakes.

Grass carp were historically used by resource managers for non-chemical control of nuisance aquatic vegetation. Initially, sterile fish were used to avoid introducing a new species, but reproducing fish made it into the mix. Today, they are widely distributed across the US and reproducing in several locations across the Upper Midwest.

Common carp received a boost in acceptance by fly fishers with the publication of *Carp Are Gamefish*

by George Von Schrader in 1990. Von Schrader's book focused on fly fishing shallow flats around the Great Lakes, and he gave specific locations for this along with flies and techniques. He was inspired by Milwaukee, Wisconsin, outdoor writer Mel Ellis, who wrote an article titled "Those Copper Colored Bones" in the July 1966 issue of *Field & Stream*.

Von Schrader's work caught the interest of Dave Whitlock, who accompanied him on several adventures. Whitlock wrote about stalking giant carp on Great Lakes flats, and the rest, as they say, is history. Carp were now a legitimate fly-rod target, and why shouldn't they be? Carp get big, fight hard, are well distributed, love to eat flies, are challenging to catch, and can be stalked and sight-fished in shallow water. They check a lot of fly fishers' boxes.

Grass carp are even more appealing, as they also jump when hooked. They are primarily vegetation

Carp are widely distributed across the waters of the Upper Midwest. They are found from the big water of the Great Lakes to tiny creeks. They are a great fly-rod target when sight-fished in the shallows. Eric Corya photo

eaters, while common carp are a lot more opportunistic. Grassies will take certain insects such as cicadas when they are abundant, but catching them consistently on a fly is still an ongoing project.

One person at the forefront of this and conducting extensive carp-catching research is Eric Corya. Based in central Indiana, Corya has several waterways close by with an abundance of common carp with grass carp mixed in. This gives him the opportunity to target these fish through the year and under varying water conditions.

Both the Pollywog and Standing Hampton can be upsized to a size 4 for use on Great Lakes flats. Feeding fish are generally targeted, but Great Lakes cruisers will move to take a fly at times. Here a bit of movement can be added to the fly to get the fish's attention, but is then stopped as the fish comes to the fly.

Mulberry trees are carp magnets when they are dropping berries. In the Upper Midwest this occurs May through July. River and lakeside mulberry tree locations are closely guarded by carp fly fishers. Normally cautious carp will rush to take a mulberry fly "plopped" underneath an active tree. Both common carp and grass carp will eagerly eat mulberries.

POLLYWOG
(Eric Corya)

- **Hook:** #6-8 60-degree jig
- **Thread:** 8/0 UNI-Thread, color to match body
- **Eyes:** Extra-small barbell, color as desired
- **Tail:** Spawn Fly Fish Polliwog Tail, with 3 mm foam disc piece slid on
- **Body:** Rayon chenille, variegated with a single turn of EP Tarantula Leg brush, color as desired

Note: The foam disc needs to be thick enough to make the tail stand upright and attract the attention of feeding carp. Pink is a favorite tail color for common carp. Grass carp regularly take the same fly in chartreuse. Smallmouth will also hit this fly.

STANDING HAMPTON
(Eric Corya)

- **Hook:** #6-8 60-degree jig
- **Thread:** 8/0 UNI-Thread, color to match body
- **Eyes:** Extra-small barbell, color as desired
- **Tail:** Ultra Chenille, with 3 mm foam disc piece slid on
- **Body:** Small Squishenille

Note: Much of the same info from the Pollywog applies to this pattern. Both should be cast several feet in front of a feeding fish and just allowed to sit and let the fish spot it. Pink and red are key tail colors.

MOJO MULBERRY
(Eric Corya)

- **Hook:** #4 Gamakatsu B10S
- **Thread:** 8/0 UNI-Thread, color to match body
- **Tail:** Green extra-fine rubber hackle
- **Body:** Black and purple Chicone's Fettuccine Foam

Note: The Fettuccine Foam is spun similar to deer hair and then trimmed to shape. This color mix is specific for mulberries. Both common carp and grass carp will target mulberries as they drop into the water. You can change colors to match leaf colors for feeding grass carp. Here you can drop the fly right on feeding fish.

Top: Nabby's Minnow, three colors; bottom: Faux Craw, three colors

Recent Rabbits

Rabbit fur is one of the most versatile and durable fly-tying materials. It can be used on or off the skin, and left natural colored or dyed a multitude of different shades. Barring and other designs can be added as well as the creation of two- and even three-tone colors.

For use in streamer-type patterns, rabbit strips are often used. Here the fur is left on the tanned skin and cut into pieces. These can be in different widths and also cut in line with or across the grain of the fur depending on the application. The uses of rabbit strip pieces are many.

The downside to using rabbit strips is that the skin soaks up a considerable amount of water,

adding extra weight to the fly. Also, the skin will eventually deteriorate after getting wet and drying multiple times. So far, there really aren't any synthetic fur substitutes that are suitable replacements for rabbit strips.

We are going to look at two different newer rabbit strip designs from a pair of talented Upper Midwest anglers/tiers. Nate Sipple is a guide with Tightlines Fly Fishing in DePere, Wisconsin. This area has a diverse range of opportunities including the trout waters of the Driftless region, countless inland waters with a diversity of species, and tributaries of both Lake Michigan and Lake Superior.

Brushes are a relatively recent material on the fly-tying scene. They are best suited to streamer applications and simplify the intricate blending of materials. These allow complex patterns to be tied quicker and easier.

Sipple's primary focus is on smallmouth bass and the nearshore waters of Lake Michigan. The flies his clients fish get a lot of hard use from constant casting and hooking aggressive fish. He refers to his Nabby's Minnow as true "guide fly"—it catches fish, stays together, and is not complicated. It has produced in both fresh and salt water for a variety of species. Nabby's Minnow is also neutrally buoyant, so fishes well on both floating and sinking-head lines.

The eyes are mounted first on the top of the hook shank about a third of the way back from the hook eye. Wire is added behind the mounted eyes to help balance the fly. Flared bucktail keeps the rabbit from fouling on the hook and adds stability to the fly while being fished.

Matt Redmond is based in northeast Ohio and has wide-ranging experience across a variety of Upper Midwest waters. His Faux Craw was created as a fleeing crayfish, but can also simulate a sculpin or goby. It has accounted for an assortment of species from smallmouth to steelhead. This pattern can also be fishing on pretty much any fly line—floating, intermediate, or sinking—based on the water depth.

In both of these patterns the use of a preformed brush to create the head greatly simplifies the tying process. Brushes also help minimize the tying time and significantly increase the durability of the fly. The combination of a brush and rabbit strip allows a nearly limitless assortment of combinations for a creative tier.

NABBY'S MINNOW

(Nate Sipple)

- **Hook:** #2/0-2 TMC 811S
- **Thread:** Black UNI Big Fly
- **Tail/belly:** Flared bucktail
- **Wing:** Rabbit strip
- **Flash:** Krystal Flash with three strands of Holographic Flashabou on each side
- **Body/head:** EP Minnow Brush
- **Eyes:** EP Game Changer Eyes
- **Weight:** .025-inch lead wire substitute, eight wraps

Note: Sipple ties this pattern in three primary colors. He recommends olive where sculpin, gobies, and lamprey are found; black when the water is off-color; and white in low, clear conditions.

FAUX CRAW

(Matt Redmond)

- **Hook:** #2 Gamakatsu B10S
- **Thread:** 140D Veevus Power Thread, color to match body
- **Eyes:** Medium barbell, secured on the top of the hook shank, just behind the eye; color as desired
- **Tail:** Three strands each of Flashabou, Holographic Flashabou, and Kreelex Flash staggered in length, sandwiched in between two sections of Extra Select Craft Fur
- **Belly:** Barred rabbit strip, with one rubber strand on each side, secured
- **Body:** 3-inch Craft Fur Brush, three to five palmered wraps, color to match tail
- **Collar:** 1.5-inch Polar Fiber Brush, three to five wraps, wrapped tight to eyes

Note: In white, gray, or silver shades, this can serve as a baitfish imitation. In rust, brown, tan, or olive combinations, it is a crayfish, goby, or sculpin. Though primarily a smallmouth fly, it has also taken largemouth bass as well as trout and pike.

STEELHEAD AND MORE

Whether we call them steelhead or migratory rainbows, they are one of the premier sportfish of the Upper Midwest and a primary target of fly anglers. This region contains a significant portion of the Great Lakes, and it's likely that all of the tributaries feeding the lakes have these rainbows in them at one time or another throughout the year.

A brief summary of these fish in the Great Lakes was presented earlier. We will review several facts to put things into proper perspective.

Rainbow trout from the McCloud River in California were stocked in the Au Sable River

A wide range of fly patterns and fly-fishing techniques will take Great Lakes steelhead. This fish hit a baitfish pattern tied on a tube. It was swung down and across current on a sink-tip line.

near Oscoda, Michigan, in 1873. These fish survived well and by the turn of the century were found all across the Great Lakes. As they are colored bright chrome while in the big lakes and when they first ascend rivers to spawn, we refer to them as "steelhead," just like their saltwater ancestors.

Great Lakes rainbows went relatively forgotten for a number of decades until the plantings of Pacific salmon in the 1960s as an effort to control invasive alewives. This brought renewed attention to the big lakes and tributaries when the salmon returned and the oversize rainbows were rediscovered. We know now that these rainbows take flies as eagerly as their saltwater-based relatives.

Today there are self-sustaining populations of these fish as well as active stocking programs to maintain populations. Various strains of migratory rainbows have been planted across the region to the point one could possibly target them 365 days a year at various locations. Steelhead account for a significant portion of the fly-fishing dollars spent across the Upper Midwest.

Migratory brown trout are also available, but in much smaller numbers and populations are much more localized. Where browns are present, they add an interesting bonus catch opportunity. Most are found in several Lake Michigan streams or coming out of Lake Ontario (technically not in the Upper Midwest).

Flies used for steelhead have gone through an interesting evolution. It was first thought they didn't hit flies at all and had to be fished with bait. Then western-style flies were used. That was followed by dead-drifting egg and nymph imitations—an extremely effective combination. We've now gone full circle and are back to swinging flies, but with patterns modified for use in this region.

The one thing the Upper Midwest / Great Lakes lacks are consistent dry-fly opportunities for steelhead. Catching a Great Lakes migratory rainbow on the surface can be done, but locations are limited and there is often a short time frame. Most of the wild fish are winter-run spring spawners and just not present when water temperatures are suitable for surface activity.

What has been done in this section is to give some additional pattern templates that are focused on steelhead. These can be combined with crossover nymph patterns from stream trout to migratory trout use as presented in the "Trout/Steelhead Crossover Nymphs" section. This is by no means a complete complement of patterns, but it does give the angler/tier a starting point for an assortment of flies that will catch migratory fish across the region.

Top: Nuke Egg, two colors; bottom: Bear's Crystal Egg, two colors

Nuke Egg

All trout and char eat fish eggs. Rainbows especially love to eat eggs. There is just too much food value in those protein-packed morsels to pass up. The eggs can be from salmon, other trout, suckers, walleye, and other species present. The imitations can range from realistic to suggestive to being true attractors to trigger the egg-eater instinct.

The Nuke Egg was one of the first egg imitations to come out of the Upper Midwest region. It was the first to go beyond the original Glo Bug and add a second material that gives the "see-through" translucent look of a real egg. Over the years it has gone through a number of updates, but the basic template has stayed the same.

Materials for the Nuke Egg are quite simple. The original pattern had a core made from a small bunch of bright Glo Bug Yarn, like flame or steelhead orange, surrounded by a thin cover of white Glo Bug Yarn. When wet, this has the appearance of an eyed egg. Various other color combinations came into the mix, some realistic while others like chartreuse over flame are attractor colors.

The original Nuke Egg still catches fish today, but fly tiers always look to change things in hopes of possibly making it better. Other materials can be used as the core or nucleus of the fly, such as various dubbings and chenille. McFly Foam came on the market and is much easier to secure and cut

A Great Lakes steelhead is safely in the net after a spirited fight. Egg patterns are a staple for the migratory rainbows of the Great Lakes. These are usually dead-drifted in combination with a nymph or small streamer.

than Glo Bug Yarn. Egg Veil is a material available through Hareline that is used to surround the core color.

Estaz and similar materials are also used to make egg imitators. These might be left plain or have a veil added. A few strands of Krystal Flash can be added as a tail to increase attraction. A fluorescent bead can add weight and color, too. This is well represented with the Crystal Egg by Bear Andrews.

Several basic rules to follow would be: When there are fish like salmon actively laying eggs, try to match the size and color, especially if the water is clear. If the water is off-color, a bit larger in size and a bit of extra flash can help. If no eggs are present, fly color can be based on water color—big, bright, and flashy in dirty water, small and muted shades in clear water.

The hook is an important component of these flies. The TMC 105 and Gamakatsu C14S are popular standard egg hooks. Personally, I like to use a heavy-wire scud hook like the Daiichi 1120. I fish Lake Erie tributaries mostly and at times have to drop down to a size 14 or smaller hook in low, clear

water. I believe the scud hooks' larger gap hooks and holds better in the smaller sizes. I also tie a lot of nymphs on the same hook, so get double use from them.

Brown trout will also feed on eggs when they are available. This is especially true in western Michigan rivers where wild brown trout will lie behind spawning salmon and enjoy the feast. Few trout will pass up an easy meal.

NUKE EGG
(Unknown)

- **Hook:** #8-14 TMC 105, Daiichi 1120, or similar heavy scud or egg hook
- **Thread:** Fluorescent orange or red 70D UTC
- **Body:** A small bunch of bright-color McFly Foam, trimmed short
- **Veil:** White or light-colored McFly Foam, Egg Veil, or similar material, surrounding the body, trimmed just past hook bend

Note: A steelhead orange color core with Oregon cheese as the veil is a great chinook egg imitation. Steelhead orange with an egg-color veil works well in the spring when steelhead and suckers are present.

BEAR'S CRYSTAL EGG
(Bear Andrews)

- **Hook:** #6-19 TMC 105 or 2457, or Daiichi 1120
- **Thread:** Red 70D UTC
- **Tail:** Pearl Krystal Flash
- **Body:** Estaz
- **Collar:** Single or multiple colors of egg yarn spread around the hook

Note: This is strictly an attractor pattern. Being highly visible, it is a good choice in the deepest, fastest flows and off-color water. Blending multiple colors here can help trigger strikes.

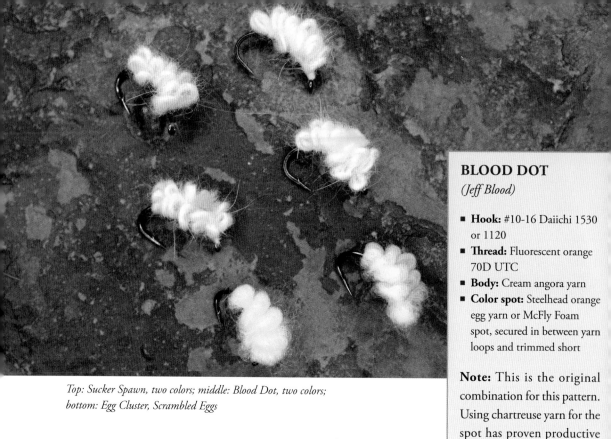

Top: Sucker Spawn, two colors; middle: Blood Dot, two colors; bottom: Egg Cluster, Scrambled Eggs

BLOOD DOT

(Jeff Blood)

- **Hook:** #10-16 Daiichi 1530 or 1120
- **Thread:** Fluorescent orange 70D UTC
- **Body:** Cream angora yarn
- **Color spot:** Steelhead orange egg yarn or McFly Foam spot, secured in between yarn loops and trimmed short

Note: This is the original combination for this pattern. Using chartreuse yarn for the spot has proven productive and is also shown.

Sucker Spawn

The name is not very glamorous, but this simple fly catches way more than its share of fish. I would venture to say that the Sucker Spawn has accounted for more Lake Erie steelhead than any other single pattern and has gained notoriety well beyond the Great lakes. Its use may have decreased a bit in recent years as the simplicity of pegging beads has become popular, but it is still a must-have pattern for the region and can be used most anywhere fish are eating eggs.

The Sucker Spawn fly originated in central Pennsylvania a number of decades ago, where it was used to target early-season trout feeding on, you guessed it, sucker eggs. It migrated to the Lake Erie tributaries in the 1980s as part of the overall growth in the Great Lakes steelhead fishery. One could even

suggest that this pattern helped put the Lake Erie tributaries on the map as "Steelhead Alley."

The original pattern was tied with cream angora yarn tied down in loops on the hook to resemble a group of sucker eggs, which are small and a pale yellow color. Red tying thread added a blood vein. So, in effect, it is a somewhat "match the hatch" concept. The angora yarn turns translucent when wet, with a very realistic look. Another factor adding to the fly's productivity is that the loops of yarn catch on the trout's teeth, making it difficult to eject. The Sucker Spawn is sometimes referred to as "the Velcro fly" because of this.

Pennsylvania guide Jeff Blood popularized the Blood Dot variation where a spot of steelhead orange egg yarn is added between the angora yarn

The waters of the Great Lakes are also home to migratory brown trout. Although less numerous than rainbows, browns can be found in all five of the Great Lakes. They will also respond to a variety of egg patterns, as well as nymphs and streamers.

loops. This gives an appearance closer to eyed trout or salmon eggs when paired with the cream angora yarn. The color of the yarn can be varied as needed to closer match natural eggs.

Various other types of yarn have been used to create different variations. A single color of egg yarn is used to make an Egg Cluster fly. Multiple egg yarn colors can be combined to make the Scrambled Eggs version. Natural egg colors can be replaced with attractor colors in off-color water conditions.

The one thing required to create all of these patterns is tying down the yarn loops correctly:

- If using a multi-ply yarn, separate a length of yarn into the individual sections. Egg yarn can be used in a single wider section of several colors combined.
- Using a heavy wet-fly or scud hook, cover the shank with thread and then tie the yarn down the length of the shank back to the hook bend.
- Bring the yarn over the top of the hook shank and secure it in a small loop.
- Now here's the key to making this fly: Lift the yarn and advance the thread directly in front of the yarn, then create another loop, slightly larger. Repeat the process until you reach the eye, where you tie off the yarn, trim it, and whip-finish.

When targeting migratory fish, be sure to use a sharp, heavy-wire wet-fly hook of some sort. The Daiichi 1530 is often used. My personal preference again lies with the scud style like the Daiichi 1120 for the wider gap hook. This is another situation where dropping size in low, clear water can produce strikes when larger offerings are ignored. Also, muted colors like the original cream, pale yellow, and pale pink are better choices in these conditions.

SUCKER SPAWN
(Unknown)

- **Hook:** #10-16 Daiichi 1120 or 1530
- **Thread:** Red 70D UTC
- **Body:** Cream angora yarn, divided into individual plies and tied in a series of loops from hook bend to eye

Note: This is the original pattern color combination. My personal favorite under good water clarity is cream yarn with chartreuse thread. This combination has also proven effective on salmon and migratory browns. Use brighter colors as water clarity decreases. Finding an assortment of colors in angora yarn may be a bit difficult. Cascade Crest (www.cascadecrest.com) has a good selection.

EGG CLUSTER AND SCRAMBLED EGGS
(Unknown)

- **Hook:** #10-16 Daiichi 1530 or 1120
- **Thread:** 70D UTC, color as desired
- **Body:** Single color (Egg Cluster) or multiple colors (Scrambled Eggs) of egg yarn or McFly Foam, tied down in loops from hook bend to eye

Note: The Egg Cluster version is often done in natural colors like egg or cheese. For the Scrambled Eggs, chartreuse / steelhead orange and steelhead orange / cheese are two of the favored colorations, but numerous combinations can be created as desired.

Grapefruit Head Leech, two colors

Grapefruit Head Leech

The use of swung flies for Great Lakes rainbows has gone through several phases. There are some references of these fish being caught on conventional streamers going back to the 1940s, but little reference to actual technique. My guess is that this was the traditional down-and-across presentation with stripping the fly back.

Based in Midland, Michigan, Scientific Anglers introduced the first modern sinking lines in 1960. Called Wet Cell, these lines were easily castable and opened the door to more-efficient presentations of streamers and wet flies in moving water. Prior to

this, lengths of lead core were added to level lines to take flies to depth.

The first book devoted to flies for these fish was *Great Lakes Steelhead Flies* by Dave Richey, published in 1979. Most of these patterns are based on traditional western ones. While these patterns caught fish, results were inconsistent.

In 1987, Scientific Anglers partnered with West Coast angler Lani Waller and released several steelhead videos filmed in the Pacific Northwest as part of their Mastery educational series. These helped to highlight the latest advances in line technology

The Grapefruit Head Leech is easily adjusted to the varying water conditions of Great Lakes tributaries. It is well recognized as a top producer across the Upper Midwest and can be tied as a shank design, on a fixed hook, and also on a tube.

and applied them to actual fishing situations. The videos spurred significant interest in this style of fishing that reached across to the Great Lakes and Upper Midwest region.

In the late 1990s, Kevin Feenstra began to apply Waller's principles to guide steelhead on his home rivers in western Michigan. Spurred by continued advances in fly lines and tying materials, over the past two decades Feenstra has refined his fly patterns and presentation techniques. More than any other single person, he helped to bring the use of two-hand rods and swung flies as a day-to-day technique for steelhead across the Great Lakes.

One of Feenstra's most recognized and most productive swung-fly patterns is the Grapefruit Head Leech. This fly has proven its worth across the Great Lakes and beyond as a top-tier fish producer. Numerous other patterns for use in the region have been created based on this design.

Feenstra is known for his intricate knowledge of the waters he fishes and his ability to blend fly design and color based on both water color and water temperature. The Grapefruit Head Leech combines key elements of a successful streamer:

color, flash, and movement. The various color combinations he uses are based on thousands of days of on-water experience. He primarily focuses on the Muskegon River system, but these principles also apply to waters across the entire Great Lakes area.

This fly was originally tied on a Daiichi 2461 hook. Feenstra changed this to a shank design with trailer hook around a decade ago. This was borrowed from the West Coast Intruder designs that allow a large-bodied fly to be tied without using a long-shank hook. The short-shank, octopus-style trailer hook minimizes leverage for a hooked fish to work free.

GRAPEFRUIT HEAD LEECH
(Kevin Feenstra)

- **Shank:** 40 mm Senyo Shank or Flymen Articulated Shank
- **Thread:** 6/0 UNI-Thread, color to match body
- **Loop:** 50-pound braid
- **Hook:** #1-2 Daiichi Octopus
- **Tail:** Black marabou, with sparse red Flashabou
- **Body:** Black marabou, palmered and tip-wrapped, with black schlappen in front
- **Wing:** Flashabou in layers; silver, then blue, topped with kelly green
- **Head:** Chartreuse Estaz or Cactus Chenille, with chartreuse Ice Dub in front
- **Eyes:** Medium silver bead chain, tied in between the two head sections (optional)

Note: Black and purple are favorite main marabou body colors. You can substitute colors as desired as well as downsize it for smaller waters. It is the basic pattern template that is most important. Feenstra has several videos and books that give insight into his various fly designs and material selections. You can get more information at www.feenstraguideservice.com.

Egg Raider, two colors

Egg Raider

As we know, trout, especially rainbow trout, love to eat eggs. Starting with simple egg patterns, this has been carried over to numerous streamer-based fly designs. Probably the most notorious of these is the Egg Sucking Leech. Created in Alaska, this is simply a Glo Bug tied in front of a Woolly Bugger and It is a deadly fly. The sight of a big leech eating a salmon egg is just more than a big Alaska rainbow trout can resist. Over the years the pattern migrated from its origin in Alaska, down through the Pacific Northwest, and finally to the Great Lakes.

The migratory rainbows of the Upper Midwest are also fond of egg-streamer combinations. Even when eggs are not present in the water, Great Lakes steelhead will take this style of fly. This is likely due to several reasons. The egg-eating instinct is just there in these fish, and the sight of something resembling an egg can be enough to trigger a strike—especially when it is attached to an additional food source. Also, the color contrast and combination from the egg-streamer duet gives increased visibility in dirty water and can also attract fish from a distance.

Greg Senyo's Egg Raider pattern is a take on these concepts. Senyo is a well-known fly creator, fly tier, angler, and material specialist, now living in southern Michigan. He grew up just outside Erie, Pennsylvania, in the heart of Steelhead Alley. This

Swung-fly use continues to grow across the Great Lakes, with the Upper Midwest area in the forefront of fly design. Tributaries of all sizes are found with several strains of fish providing a long-lived opportunity to target steelhead across the region.

gave him a front seat to some of the best migratory trout fishing found anywhere and an open classroom to experiment with a wide range of fly designs and materials to catch these fish.

While most of the Great Lakes tributaries lack the oversize leeches found in many of Alaska's rivers, there is an abundance of different baitfish in these waters. Creek chubs, emerald shiners, juvenile trout, madtoms, and more are found across the Upper Midwest. When there are spawning fish and eggs in the water, they are going to capitalize on this food source. Steelhead are the primary predator when they enter many systems, and the sight of a smaller fish going for eggs ignites their killer instinct.

The heart of the Egg Raider is an 8 mm plastic bead. This is normally an orange shade when spawning fish are present, but other colors such as chartreuse can be used for visibility and contrast

if no eggs are present. This is slid to the front of the shank used for the fly. A wire or braid loop is attached and an octopus-style hook slipped on the loop after the fly is completed.

The main part starts with a rabbit strip tail, and a sequence of additional materials per the recipe completes the fly. It can be tied as a full attractor in bright colors, in a natural color scheme to imitate a specific organism, or in a color combination to contrast with the bead. Time of year and water clarity help determine this.

The Egg Raider can be fished behind a sink tip or long leader with split shot. It is swung behind spawning fish or through suspected holding water. Strikes are usually strong and aggressive, so hang on!

SENYO'S EGG RAIDER 2.0
(Greg Senyo)

- **Shank:** 26 mm Aqua Round Eye Shank, cut to slip on bead
- **Bead:** Mottled orange 8 mm
- **Thread:** Black 8/0 Veevus
- **Loop:** Senyo Intruder Wire
- **Hook:** #2-4 octopus style
- **Eyes:** Medium Hareline Dubbin Dumbbell Pseudo Eyes
- **Tail/shoulder:** Black Hareline Dubbin Rabbit Strip
- **Flash:** Copper Flashabou
- **Body:** EP Senyo Chromatic Brush "garbage loop" sandwiched with ostrich and flash fibers of choice
- **Head:** Ice Dub

Note: The primary targets for this pattern are Great Lakes steelhead and salmon, migratory brown trout, and char in Alaska. Favorite color combinations are fuchsia/purple/pink, olive/brown/copper, olive/copper/gold, black/purple/blue, and white/olive/pearl. Schultz Outfitters has a YouTube video with Senyo showing how to tie the Egg Raider.

Crafty Leech Tube Fly, four color variations

Crafty Leech Tube Fly

Versatility in fly patterns is a key to consistent steelhead success. We often think of this primarily in terms of size and color, but the hooking capability of the fly is also a consideration. Just as we adjust a fly for size and color depending on conditions, there are times when the size or style of hook can be altered for the situation.

This is where the use of a tube fly comes into play. Here the fly is tied on some sort of a hollow tube. The tippet is run through the tube and a hook is attached. The hook may be seated into the tube by a junction piece and functions similar to a conventional fly. It can also be secured with a loop and set back behind the fly body as with a shank design. If the hook is damaged, it is easily replaced without discarding the fly. When unhooking a fish, the fly is easily moved up the leader and out of the way, minimizing the possibility of damage to both fish and fly. The benefits of tube flies are many.

Tube flies have a strong following in Europe, where they originated back in the 1940s. The tubes themselves are often plastic. If a weighted fly is wanted, the tube can be metal, usually aluminum, brass, or copper that has a plastic liner to

Many of the Great Lakes tributaries of the Upper Midwest vary in flow rate and water color based on rain and snowmelt and are referred to as "spate streams." Flow color and size is often based on water clarity so that the fly is visible to the fish. Various color schemes are more productive than others based on the water clarity.

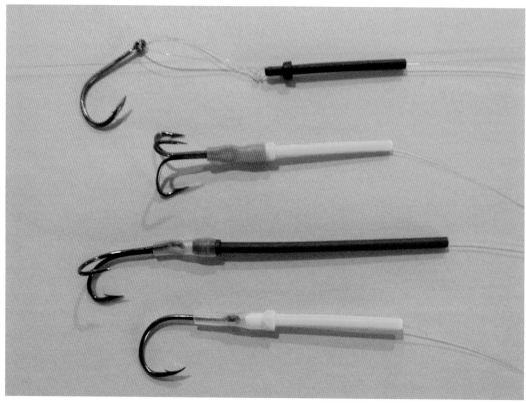

Different hook setup options with tube flies. The hook can be secured into a junction that connects it to the fly tube, or can be extended beyond the tube on a loop from the tippet. Double and treble hooks can also be used.

prevent damage to the tippet. There are also cones and beads sized to fit on tubes. The fly is then tied on the tube. This is best suited to streamer-style patterns, but can be done with large nymphs, too.

A vise dedicated just to tubes is not necessary. Special tapered adapters are available that clamp into a standard vise to hold the tube and keep it from spinning while tying. You may even be able to find a regular needle of some sort that will be adequate to secure the tube and allow you to tie a handful of tube flies.

Jeff Liskay and I are strong proponents of using tube patterns to swing for steelhead. This is especially true on the Lake Erie tributaries where the fly is constantly passing over shale ledges. By placing an octopus-style hook inverted on the loop, so that the hook rides up, snags are minimized. Dropping hook size to a 4 or even a 6 will also reduce snags. A fish or two may be lost on the smaller hook, but that is the tradeoff for fly preservation.

The Crafty Leech Tube Fly presented here is the basic pattern template we have used successfully for a number of years. Extra Select Craft Fur is the heart of the fly. We already know the versatility of this material. It is super durable and available in a full spectrum of colors to match any water condition.

The tail of the fly and main wing are Extra Select Craft Fur. The tail can be tied in flat or reverse-tied. The main wing is reverse-tied or propped by other materials to maintain profile. If the tail is tied in flat, the final length will be a bit longer. Reverse-tying the tail decreases the length.

The body is Flat Diamond Braid or Ice Dub. Flash can be heavy or sparse in the main wing; the collar is schlappen and then finished with a veil of Ice Dub or Senyo Laser Dub. The fly is not very technical. It is mainly getting the three primary components—color, flash, and movement—in sync with the water conditions.

A short-shank hook is used. A straight-eye design is fine when the hook is being set into a junction piece. If set back on a loop, an octopus style is best. Sizes generally run from 2 to 6.

I hate to get too specific on colors, as everyone seems to have their favorites. Here are a few basic starting points: In tannic water with visibility, mixes of olive and brown with flash blends of copper, gold, and kelly green are productive. Olive with an olive/copper flash blend and chartreuse veil at the front is good in clear water.

When water temp goes below 40 degrees F, try black with blue. In off-color conditions, make the fly visible: black and flame or black and cerise. In the spring, white/blue and white/chartreuse combos work well for drop-back fish targeting salmon fry and other baitfish. If I was limited to only a single color combo to fish in all conditions, it would be purple and chartreuse. Another consistent color combo is black and red.

CRAFTY LEECH TUBE FLY
(Jeff Liskay)

- **Tube:** Plastic tube approximately 2½ inches long; melt the end going on the adapter so there is a small lip on the tube
- **Thread:** 140D UTC, color to match body
- **Tail:** Extra Select Craft Fur, tied in flat or reverse-tied
- **Body:** Flat Diamond Braid, ribbed with fine wire or monofilament to help strengthen it, or Ice Dub but keep it thin
- **Wing:** Extra Select Craft Fur, reverse-tied, with mixed colors of Flashabou or your favorite flash material
- **Collar:** Schlappen
- **Eyes:** Bead chain or barbell (optional)
- **Veil/head:** Ice Dub or Senyo's Laser Dub, usually a contrasting color to rest of fly

Note: The overall length of this fly usually works out to around 3 inches. It can be upsized a bit for big water or off-color conditions. After whip-finishing the head, cut the tube close to the head and melt a lip on the end, then coat the thread. Several shops in the Upper Midwest carry tube fly components. The various ways to set up the hook on a tube pattern are shown in the photo on page 124.

A number of straight-eye bait hooks can be used to set into the junction piece. The Gamakatsu B10S is becoming popular in this role because it is strong and holds fish extremely well. When placing the hook in a loop to ride back farther, Octopus hooks are often favored. This style is available from several manufacturers. In both hook styles, sizes 2 through 6 are most often used and can be adjusted as needed.

Grim Reaper, four colors

Bonus Fly: The Grim Reaper

Subsurface patterns focused primarily on large-mouth bass are a bit unique. We generally think of largemouth on a fly in terms of surface patterns. This is the classic view of fly fishing for largemouth and is certainly a big part of this fishing. But as we know, most fish do the bulk of their feeding subsurface, and largemouth bass are no exception.

Pat Ehler's Grim Reaper takes the "jig and pig" concept of gear fishermen and puts it into a fly format. This produces a fly that can be cast and let settle in heavy cover such as openings in lily pads and brush.

You can use several different lines to fish the fly. Around lily pads a floating line and short leader is best, as it gives the fly a more upward hop on the retrieve and minimizes line catching the pads. Around docks and fallen trees a sink-tip might be best to keep the fly down along the bottom for a longer time. To fish deeper cover such as ledges, drop-offs, or deep brush, a full-sink line might be best.

The leader should be strong and abrasion resistant, as this fly is designed to fish in cover and pull fish out when they are hooked. Twenty-pound fluorocarbon is not too heavy, as it allows you to put

Largemouth bass are one of the most widely distributed fish in North America. They are easily accessed by many anglers across the Upper Midwest and provide a variety of fly-fishing opportunities. More subsurface patterns for largemouth, like the Grim Reaper, are coming into play. Pat Ehlers photo

pressure on a hooked fish and minimize losing flies if you get hung up. An 8-weight would be the lightest outfit to use, with a 9-weight or maybe even a 10-weight better suited depending on where you are fishing.

The fly weight and size can be varied depending on the area being fished. The Grim Reaper is commercially tied on a size 3/0 hook with a focus on largemouth. Large painted lead eyes provide the weight. There is a lot of material on this size hook, so a heavier fly line makes casting easier. This fly is designed to be fished in lake cover where casting accuracy and fly placement is often more important than distance.

The precut Reaper Tails are made from a high-grade Ultrasuede material and are available through www.theflyfishers.com. Pat Cohen's Wiggle Tails from Hareline can also be used, as they are pretty much the same thing. You can also cut your own from craft store Ultrasuede, which can

be colored with markers. There are different grades of Ultrasuede; the precut ones are made from premium material.

Without the specific Reaper Tails, thinking outside the box can give some ideas for a suitable substitute. A regular rabbit strip can be used, or something like Mangum's Dragon Tails. The point here is that if the original material is not at hand, options may exist. Sometimes these experiments work, sometimes not—but they are always worth a try.

The Grim Reaper is available commercially in a full spectrum of colors for use in different conditions. In off-color conditions, black/purple would be the first choice for visibility in dirty water. As clarity improves, the shift would be to more-natural shades. Here the "dark day / dark color, bright day / bright color" adage also applies.

It has also proven to be a versatile pattern. Though designed for largemouth, the Grim Reaper will also take big smallmouth, northern pike, muskie, and even steelhead and salmon. In the salt it works well for redfish, and Ehler also ties a downsized version in colors for bonefish.

GRIM REAPER
(Pat Ehlers)

- **Hook:** #3/0 Gamakatsu 60-degree EWG jig
- **Thread:** 6/0 UNI-Thread, color to match body
- **Tail:** Reaper Tail
- **Body:** UV Polar Chenille
- **Legs:** Sili Legs

Note: Be sure to fish this fly on a loop knot for maximum movement. Also, fish will often hit it on the drop, so be ready to set the hook at all times.

APPENDIX A:
IMPORTANT
TYING STEPS

How to Tie the Parallel Deer Hair Body

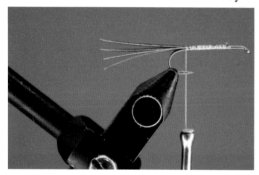

Start the thread and cover the hook shank with thread. Secure three or four pheasant tail fibers to the top of the hook shank. The fibers should extend back approximately the length of the hook shank.

Cut a section of deer body hair approximately ¼ inch in diameter for a size 10 hook. Remove all

the fuzz and even the tips of the hair in a hair tamper, and pull out any short hair. Measure the length of the hook shank from the hair tips forward. Move the section of hair back so the tips extend just past the bend of the hook and the hair is around the hook shank.

Secure the hair a bit behind the hook eye. Wrap the thread back in even spirals to the bend of the hook. Take a few wraps at the bend, then wrap forward in spirals. This should create a series of X wraps securing the hair around the hook shank.

Trim the butt ends of the deer hair and cover with thread. Regular wings and/or hackle can be added at this point. If a separate upright wing post is being used as in the Roberts Drake, add this first. The deer hair body can be tied in behind this.

Tying a Regan Spinner Pattern

Create the body as described in parallel deer hair body instructions, this time leaving the deer hair butt ends exposed in the front. Pull the exposed butt ends straight up and secure them in place. Wrap the thread around the base of the hair to create a parachute post to wrap hackle. Trim the ends of the hair even.

Prepare feather tip wings so they are about the length of the hook shank. Secure these in front of the upright post hair so the shiny side of the feather is up.

After trimming away the feather stem, separate the wing feathers and secure them with a series of thread X wraps so they extend perpendicular to the hook shank. The feathers should be shiny side up, dull side down. Put a drop of superglue at the base of the feathers to add extra strength.

Secure a hackle at the base of the upright post, then wrap from the feather downward around the post five or six times to form the parachute hackle. Tie off the hackle in front of the wings and trim. Cut the upright post hairs evenly just above the parachute hackle.

The finished Regan Spinner.

Using Zuddy's Leg Puller

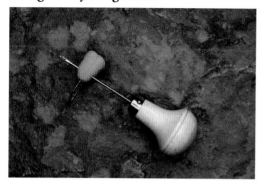

Push the end of the Leg Puller through the foam body where you want the legs, keeping it as level as possible. If the puller is hard to start or sticking, a tiny amount of Vaseline or silicone paste will help.

After the Leg Puller is back out of the foam body, pull the rubber legs free. You can then pull the rubber legs through the body by hand and trim each side evenly to the desired length.

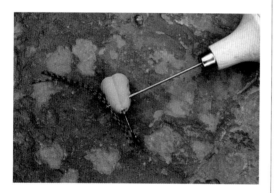

After the Leg Puller is through the body, insert the tips of the rubber legs through the hole in the end of the puller. Slowly bring the Leg Puller with the rubber legs back through the body.

APPENDIX B: ADDITIONAL FLY PATTERN RECIPES

LIGHTHOUSE SLATE WING OLIVE

(Dennis Potter)

- **Hook:** #18-20 TMC 101
- **Thread:** White 50D Benecchi Ultra Strong
- **Tail:** Dun Bett's Tailing Fibers or Microfibetts
- **Abdomen:** Light olive 8/0 UNI-Thread
- **Thorax:** Light olive Spirit River Fine & Dry Dubbing
- **Wing:** Gray EP Silky Fibers
- **Indicator:** Fluorescent pink or fluorescent yellow EP Fibers

LIGHTHOUSE HENDRICKSON DUN

(Dennis Potter)

- **Hook:** #14 TMC 100
- **Thread:** Tan or light gray 8/0 UNI-Thread
- **Tail:** Dun Bett's Tailing Fibers or Microfibetts
- **Abdomen:** Hendrickson Pink Spirit River Fine & Dry UV Dubbing
- **Thorax:** Hendrickson Pink Spirit River Fine & Dry UV Dubbing
- **Wing:** Gray EP Silky Fibers
- **Indicator:** Fluorescent pink or fluorescent yellow EP Fibers

Note: The Lighthouse patterns can cover different mayfly species by altering hook size and body color. Potter uses the fluorescent pink indicator on the wing for the daytime-hatching mayflies. For those fished in the evening and into dark, he uses the fluorescent yellow, as it is much easier to see in low light. This is great tip to follow and can be utilized on all kinds of surface flies.

MCCOY BOONDOGGLE SPINNER—BROWN DRAKE

(Ed McCoy)

- **Hook:** #12-14 Gamakatsu B10S
- **Thread:** Rusty brown 6/0 UNI-Thread
- **Tail:** Moose body hair
- **Body:** Cream 2 mm sheet foam, colored with Prismacolor canary yellow and dark brown on top
- **Hackle:** One cree and one grizzly dyed golden straw
- **Wing:** Whitetail deer belly hair

MCCOY BOONDOGGLE SPINNER—HEX

(Ed McCoy)

- **Hook:** #8 Gamakatsu B10S Stinger
- **Thread:** Yellow 6/0 UNI-Thread
- **Tail:** Moose body hair
- **Body:** Cream 2 mm sheet foam, colored with Prismacolor canary yellow with dark brown on top
- **Hackle:** One cree and one grizzly dyed golden straw
- **Wing:** Whitetail deer belly hair

MCCOY BOONDOGGLE SPINNER— *ISONYCHIA*

(Ed McCoy)

- **Hook:** #12-14 Gamakatsu B10S Stinger
- **Thread:** Iron gray 6/0 UNI-Thread
- **Tail:** Moose body hair
- **Body:** Gray or burgundy 2 mm sheet foam, colored with Prismacolor warm grey on sides
- **Hackle:** Two dark dun
- **Wing:** Whitetail deer belly hair

SWINGIN' D

(Mike Schultz)

- **Rear hook:** #4 Gamakatsu B10S
- **Thread:** UTC 140, color to match body
- **Tail:** Two saddle hackles with Flashabou
- **Rear body:** Senyo Predator Wrap, with a collar of rabbit fur cut from hide and spun in a loop
- **Connector:** 30- to 40-pound coated wire, with three 6 mm plastic beads
- **Front hook:** #2/0 Gamakatsu Worm Hook
- **Front body:** Wrapped rabbit strip, then Senyo Predator Wrap; secure the glass rattle and cover with Predator Wrap
- **Rattle:** Large glass
- **Sides:** Grizzly saddle, one on each side
- **Throat:** Mirror Wrap
- **Collar:** Marabou, tip wrapped
- **Head:** Large Rainy's Diver Head

Note: The original color scheme for the Swingin' D was white with red Mirror Wrap and marabou. White/olive is another popular combination, along with chartreuse. Be sure to glue the diver head securely so it stays level and doesn't twist.

MINI SWINGIN' D

(Mike Schultz)

- **Rear hook:** Replace with 20 mm Fish Spine
- **Thread:** White 70D UTC

- **Rear body:** Two saddle hackles with Flashabou, Palmer Chenille, and wrapped rabbit strip, topped with mallard flank
- **Connector:** 30-pound coated wire with one 6 mm 3D bead
- **Front hook:** #1/0-1 Partridge Universal Predator
- **Front body:** Wrapped rabbit strip, small rattle, with Palmer Chenille over top
- **Collar:** Tip-wrapped marabou, grizzly saddle each side, Senyo Predator Wrap, and large Palmer Chenille
- **Head:** Small Rainy's Foam Diver Head

Note: As with the Mini D&D, this version is a bit easier to throw and better suited to smaller water and when the fish are on smaller bait. Color schemes should be similar to the larger version, and add an all-black version, too. Use it for both smallmouth and trout.

LEGGY BOI

(Mike Schultz)

- **Thread:** 140D UTC, color to match body
- **Tail section:** 15 mm Fish Spine, marabou, one set rubber legs each side, and hen saddle hackle
- **First body section:** 15 mm Fish Spine, 1-inch Translucy Fly Brush, two sets rubber legs each side, and hen saddle hackle
- **Rear hook:** #4 Ahrex 274 Gammarus, with 23 mm Senyo Trout Shank with loop cut off secured, wrapped with 1-inch Translucy Fly Brush, two sets rubber legs each side, and hen saddle hackle
- **Front body section:** 25 mm Fish Spine, repeat process—1-inch Translucy Fly Brush, two sets legs, and hen saddle hackle—two times
- **Front hook:** #1/0-1 Ahrex S280 Minnow, with 23 mm Senyo shank secured per above, tungsten bead, 2-inch Translucy Fly Brush, two sets rubber legs, webby rooster saddle behind tungsten bead, and Crustaceous Brush in front of bead

Note: The buoyancy of this fly is controlled by the weight of the tungsten bead and the amount of Cretaceous Brush used. It is tied in different attractor shades as desired. This is the standard smallmouth size. Tie with larger hooks if specifically targeting pike.

5150
(Tanner Ehlers)

- **Hook:** #4 Ahrex FW550
- **Bead:** 7/32-inch or 6 mm tungsten slotted
- **Thread:** 140D UTC, color to match body
- **Tail:** Wapsi Fly Tail
- **Rear sections:** 12 mm articulated shank with ¼-inch foam cylinder section
- **Body:** UV Polar Chenille
- **Collar:** Blood quill marabou, wrapped

Note: The commercial version of this pattern is in solid base colors: white, chartreuse, black, purple, olive, brown. With barred marabou and creative work on the foam cylinders with a Sharpie, a wide range of custom looks can be created.

RABBIT STRIP DIVER
(Larry Dahlberg)

- **Hook:** #2/0-4 Gamakatsu B10S
- **Thread:** 140D UTC, color to match body
- **Weedguard:** 20- to 25-pound stiff mono, or nyloncoated wire if targeting toothy predators (optional)
- **Tail:** Rabbit strip, standard size for hooks up to #1, magnum for #1/0-2/0, with Flashabou or Krystal Flash
- **Collar:** Deer belly hair, color as desired, trimmed to shape with hair tips left in
- **Head:** Deer belly hair, color as desired, trimmed to shape

Note: White, black, and olive are favorite colors for this pattern. Tie in a sizable collar, as this helps create a vortex when stripped and increases the movement of the rabbit. The collar can be stiffened by coating it with flexible adhesive, such as Flexament.

MEGA DIVER
(Larry Dahlberg)

- **Hook:** #3/0-5/0 Gamakatsu or Owner Worm Hook with built-in weedguard
- **Thread:** White 100D GSP
- **Tail/wing:** Big Fly Fiber with Flashabou mixed in; optional: add several long grizzly saddle feathers or additional flash material

- **Collar:** Deer belly hair, trimmed with hair tips left in
- **Head:** Deer belly hair, trimmed to shape; coat bottom with cement to add strength
- **Eyes:** 3D, sized to hook (optional)

Note: To simplify the tying process with the required larger hook, the conventional plastic worm hooks work well. Adding the grizzly saddles and eyes gives an updated look to the pattern. This classic pattern is often overlooked these days, but is still a great fish-catching design.

EXO SKIN CLAWDAD
(Eric Corya)

- **Hook:** #2-4 3XL-4XL streamer
- **Thread:** 140D UTC, color to match body
- **Eyes:** Barbell
- **Head:** Squishenille, wrapped from halfway around hook bend to just across from hook point
- **Claws:** Cut from Kiley's Exo Skin, attached as in the regular Clawdad
- **Body:** Squishenille, wrapped to form body and around eyes

Note: The updated materials allow for a wide range of color options and give natural feel when picked up by a fish.

SWING CRAW
(Dave Pynczkowski)

- **Hook:** #4 Gamakatsu B10 or TMC 200R
- **Thread:** Brown or olive 140D UTC
- **Eyes:** Medium or large barbell, in chartreuse or orange
- **Tail:** Four sets of Sili Legs, tied secured at middle and folded over, trim top four legs
- **Belly:** Tan Extra Select Craft Fur
- **Legs:** Two sets of Sili Legs per side, tied down in middle and folded over and secured
- **Back:** Medium brown or olive Extra Select Craft Fur, butt ends left exposed and trimmed even, mottled coloring added with permanent marker

Note: For saltwater fans, tie this on a stainless hook, add a bit of flash, and adjust the colors a bit for a fun bonefish and redfish fly!

The Sulphur Dun mayfly, Ephemerella invaria, *also called the Pale Evening Dun or Light Hendrickson. This long-lasting hatch is a favorite of anglers across both Midwest and eastern US trout waters. They are closely related to the Pale Morning Dun of the western states,* Ephemerella infrequens. *The same patterns can be used for both hatches. Kevin Feenstra photo*

INDEX